I.

# CHINESE VEGETARIAN Dishes

## Nim Chee Lee

WINDWARD

Published by Windward, an imprint owned by
W.H. Smith & Son Limited

Registered No. 237811 England

Trading as WHS Distributors,
St John's House, East Street, Leicester LE1 6NE

© Marshall Cavendish Limited 1986

ISBN 0 7112-0430-6

Printed and bound in Hong Kong by
Dai Nippon Printing Co

# INTRODUCTION

Chinese cooking and vegetarian cooking; two extremely popular types of cuisine that are combined here in a delicious selection of recipes. Most Westerners have become dedicated followers of Chinese food over the last few decades, attracted by its tasty appeal, quick preparation and appetising appearance, and even those people who are not committed vegetarians have come to realize that good health is not, after all, based on eating large daily quantities of meat. If vegetarian meals are incorporated into the week's menus, so much the better for variety, and if those vegetarian meals are based on Chinese methods of cooking, the results are both delicious and nutritious

The Chinese have long appreciated the value of vegetables – both nutritionally and aesthetically – in their daily fare. In addition, their eating habits follow a pattern that is particularly suitable for vegetarian cuisine – the practice of combining several dishes in one meal, rather than having a substantial main course with a couple of small vegetable accompaniments. This makes much more sense for a meatless meal, which ideally should feature a number of complementary courses of equal importance. To help you make a selection, recipes of different basic types are combined on the following pages, rather than following a rigorous section-by-section chapter division. However, so that you can see at a glance which section any particular recipe does belong to, the contents list on the following pages groups recipes under their general heading.

A very exciting element in this book is that the recipes are truly and authentically Chinese – using Chinese ingredients and the wonderful methods of cooking – stir-frying and steaming – which the Chinese have perfected; methods which help to retain the appearance and the nutritional value of the vegetables. Because of the authenticity, many of the vegetables will be strange to you, but an illustrated key on pages 118 and 119 will help you to identify just what it is you are looking for! Where possible, better-known European substitutes are suggested, but bear in mind that if you use these substitutes, the taste of the dish *will* be different, and probably less authentic.

It is worth making special sorties into those areas of the many big cities where the Chinese communities live, and searching through the shops for the special ingredients. Do not be afraid to ask for assistance; the Chinese are notoriously friendly people and will be only too willing to help. So, do not be put off by a recipe because of the alien nature of the ingredients; remember that these ingredients are common everyday ones to the Chinese, and that you will find the great majority of them in almost any Chinese supermarket or store.

*Chinese Vegetarian Dishes* offers the cook and gourmet an easy introduction into authentic Chinese cookery, together with a host of delicious recipes, beautifully illustrated, that will appeal to vegetarians and meat-eaters alike.

# CONTENTS

# 奶汁冬瓜帽

## Winter Melon Pieces with Milk

**INGREDIENTS** (SERVES 4)

450 g/1 lb winter melon
8-10 Chinese mushrooms
3 spiced bean curds
6-8 button mushrooms
3 tblspns corn oil
125 ml/4 fl oz milk
1½ tblspns cornflour

**SEASONING A**
50-75 ml/2-3 fl oz clear soup
    stock (see p. 116)
1 slice fresh root ginger
½ tspn salt
½ tspn white pepper

**SEASONING B**
1 tspn salt
1 tspn sugar
½ tspn white pepper

**METHOD**

**1**  Cut away the skin from the winter melon and discard the seeds. Chop the flesh into rectangular pieces about 5 mm × 4 cm/¼ × 1½ inches. Place these in a large bowl and add seasoning **A**. Put the bowl in a steamer and steam for 20 minutes. Drain off the liquid and reserve it, but discard the ginger.
**2**  Soak the Chinese mushrooms in boiling water for 20 minutes. Wash the bean curds and button mushrooms. Cut off and discard the stalks from the Chinese mushrooms, then chop the caps very finely with the bean curds and button mushrooms. Sprinkle over seasoning **B** and mix everything together well.
**3**  Heat the oil in a wok and stir-fry the Chinese mushroom mixture for 2 minutes. Press this on top of the winter melon. Steam for 15 minutes more, then remove and turn the bowl upside-down on a plate.
**4**  Mix together the milk, the liquid drained from the melon and the cornflour. Pour into a small pan and bring to the boil slowly, stirring all the time. Let the mixture bubble for a minute or so until it thickens, then pour it over the winter melon and serve at once.

# 冰心玉潔

## Crystal Beauty

**INGREDIENTS** (SERVES 4)

1 section lotus root
½ packet condensed
    agar-agar powder
450 ml/¾ pint clear soup
    stock (see p. 116)
maraschino cherries, to serve

**SEASONING**
1½ tspns salt
½ tspn white pepper

**METHOD**

**1**  Peel the lotus root and chop into small pieces. Soak these in water for 30 minutes.
**2**  Put the agar-agar powder into a pan with the stock and the seasoning. Simmer gently for 30 minutes, then remove from the heat. Strain through a sieve lined with a piece of muslin.
**3**  Drain the lotus root and put it into the strained liquid. Tip back into the rinsed out pan and bring to the boil. Pour into a square loaf tin, cover with cling film, and when cool, put in the refrigerator.
**4**  When ready to serve, remove the tin from the refrigerator – it should have set into a firm jelly. Cut into strips and serve with ice cubes and maraschino cherries.

**NOTE**
This dish is a delightfully fresh one to serve on a hot summer's day.

# 韭花銀芽

# *Chive Flowers with Bean Sprouts*

### INGREDIENTS (SERVES 4)

50 g/2 oz chives with flowers
350 g/12 oz bean sprouts
4 tblspns corn oil

### SEASONING

⅔ tspn salt
1 tblspn light soy sauce
½ tspn white pepper

### METHOD

**1**  Wash the chives. Discard any old or withered stems and chop the remainder into 2.5-cm/1-inch pieces.
**2**  Chop off the ends of the bean sprouts. Wash the remainder clean and dry in a clean cloth.
**3**  Heat the oil in a wok and stir-fry the chives and bean sprouts with the seasoning over a high heat for 1 minute. Serve at once.

### NOTES

**1**  This is a fresh attractive-looking dish which is also very nutritious.
**2**  Although the chives shown here are rather broader-stemmed than those commonly grown in the U.K., ordinary chives would be perfectly suitable for this recipe and the one below. Pick them just as the flower buds have appeared.

# 炸韭菜结

# *Fried Chive Knots*

### INGREDIENTS (SERVES 4)

100 g/4 oz wheat flour
⅓ tspn salt
2 tblspns potato starch
2 eggs, beaten
approx 175 ml/6 fl oz water
225 g/8 oz chives (without flowers)
1 pan of corn oil for deep frying

### SEASONING

3 tblspns dark soy sauce
½ tblspn chilli sauce
½ tblspn sugar
1 tspn garlic powder

### METHOD

**1**  Mix together the wheat flour, salt and potato starch in a large bowl. Make a well in the centre and tip in the beaten eggs. Stir, adding the water gradually, to incorporate the flour, keeping the mixture smooth. Add sufficient water to make a batter the consistency of thick cream.
**2**  Discard any old or withered leaves from the chives and wash the remainder. Scald a handful of chives in boiling water to soften them.
**3**  Divide the remainder of the chives into bundles of 3. Fold these into 7.5-cm/3-inch long sections and bind them together with the softened chives.
**4**  Coat the bundles of chives in the batter, making sure they are evenly covered. Fry a few at a time in the hot oil until golden brown. Drain on absorbent paper while you cook the remainder.
**5**  Cut the knots into diagonal slices and serve with the seasoning mixed together in a small bowl.

# 盛世太平火鍋
## Dish of the Flourishing

### INGREDIENTS (SERVES 4)

8 Chinese mushrooms
2 bundles vermicelli
½ a salted or preserved
  vegetable
350 g/12 oz spinach
1 bamboo shoot
4 tblspns corn oil
2 tblspns finely chopped
  shallot
1 tblspn light soy sauce
1.5 litres/2½ pints clear soup
  stock (see p. 116)
10 pieces triangular shaped
  fried bean curds
100 g/4 oz dried bean curds
100 g/4 oz fungus slices

### SEASONING

2 tspns salt
1 tspn white pepper

### METHOD

**1**   Soak the Chinese mushrooms in boiling water for 20 minutes. Drain. Cut off and discard the stalks. Soak the vermicelli in cold water for 20 minutes. Drain and cut into 2.5-cm/1-inch sections.
**2**   Wash the salted or preserved vegetable. Discard outer skin, then cut into thin slices.
**3**   Discard any old or withered leaves from the spinach. Scrape off the dirt and rootlets from the spinach root, but do not chop off the root itself. Wash the spinach well and chop.
**4**   Wash the bamboo shoot and cut into slices.
**5**   Heat the oil in a wok and stir-fry the shallot until browned. Add the soy sauce, soup stock, fried bean curds, dried bean curd, the fungus, bamboo shoot and salted vegetable slices, the Chinese mushrooms and half of the seasoning. Bring to the boil.
**6**   Add the vermicelli and spinach with the rest of the seasoning and boil for 2 minutes more. Transfer to an earthenware pot and serve.

### NOTE
This dish is so-called because very good weather conditions are necessary to produce all the vegetables at the same time.

# 興子旺孫暖鍋
## Pot of Prosperity

### INGREDIENTS (SERVES 4)

175 g/6 oz Chinese
  mushrooms
3 corn-on-the-cobs
175 g/6 oz green beans
50 g/2 oz mange tout
225 g/8 oz straw mushrooms
175 g/6 oz button mushrooms
175 g/6 oz abalone
  mushrooms
175 g/6 oz long-stem
  mushrooms
1 large onion
4-6 tblspns corn oil
75 g/3 oz plain flour
1.5 litres/2½ pints clear
  soup stock (see p. 116)

### SEASONING

2 tspns salt
½ tspn white pepper
1 tblspn sugar
½ tspn finely chopped fresh
  root ginger

### METHOD

**1**   Soak the Chinese mushrooms in boiling water for 20 minutes. Drain. Cut off and discard stalks.
**2**   Cut off and discard the outer leaves and feathery parts of the corns. Wash the cobs and chop into 2.5-cm/1-inch sections.
**3**   Wash the beans and mange tout. Rub off the membranes from the beans, and top and tail the mange tout.
**4**   Wash all the mushrooms, then cut off and discard the stalks. Finely chop the onion.
**5**   Heat the oil in a wok and stir-fry the onion until lightly browned. Mix together the flour and soup, adding the liquid gradually to the flour to keep it smooth. Pour this into the pan with the onion and bring to the boil over medium heat, stirring all the time. Add the seasoning.
**6**   Add all the vegetable ingredients and boil for 2 minutes more. Transfer to an earthenware pot and serve.

### NOTES
**1**   Substitute 100 g/4 oz shredded bamboo shoots for the long-stem mushrooms.
**2**   Substitute 100 g/4 oz fresh dark-gilled mushrooms for the abalone mushrooms.

# Stuffed Cucumber

素釀大黃瓜

## INGREDIENTS (SERVES 4)

6 Chinese mushrooms
1 large cucumber
1 tblspn cornflour
50-75 g/2-3 oz water
   chestnuts
1 small carrot
½ a salted cabbage root
1 bean curd
5 tblspns corn oil
1½ tspns sesame oil
1.2 litres/2 pints clear soup
   stock (see p. 116)

### SEASONING A

⅔ tspn salt
½ tspn mustard powder
1 tblspn cornflour
1 egg white

### SEASONING B

1 tspn salt
½ tspn white pepper

## METHOD

**1**  Soak the Chinese mushrooms in boiling water for 20 minutes. Drain. Cut off and discard the stalks.
**2**  Cut off and discard the end parts of the cucumber. Peel and chop into 2.5-cm/1-inch round sections. Scoop out the seeds. Wash the cucumber rings and wipe dry on absorbent paper. Dust the inside with the cornflour.
**3**  Peel the water chestnuts and carrot. Remove outer pieces of cabbage root. Wash all these ingredients then chop them very finely, together with the Chinese mushrooms.
**4**  Blanch the bean curd in boiling water for 3 minutes. Mash it and drain off the water. Blend with the chopped ingredients, together with seasoning **A**. Mix everything together thoroughly.
**5**  Heat the oil in a wok and stir-fry the mixture for 2 minutes. Pack into the cucumber rings.
**6**  Tip the oil from the wok into a frying pan and fry the stuffed cucumber rings over a medium heat until lightly browned. Pour the soup stock over them and bring to the boil. Lower the heat and simmer very gently for 20 minutes. Add seasoning **B** and the sesame oil. Transfer to a serving dish and serve.

---

釀金錢

# Stuffed Chinese Mushrooms

## INGREDIENTS (SERVES 4)

16-20 large Chinese
   mushrooms
1 tblspn cornflour
1 bean curd
2 tblspns water chestnuts
1 small carrot
¼ a salted vegetable
8 tblspns corn oil
16-20 green beans

### SEASONING A

½ tspn white pepper
½ tspn salt
1 tspn sugar
1 tblspn cornflour

### SEASONING B

1½ tblspns light soy sauce
1 tspn sugar
3 tblspns clear soup stock
   (see p. 116)
⅓ tspn salt

## METHOD

**1**  Soak the Chinese mushrooms in boiling water for 20 minutes. Drain. Cut off and discard the stalks, then coat the inner sides with the cornflour.
**2**  Wash the bean curd, water chestnuts, carrot and salted vegetable. Peel the water chestnuts and the carrot, then chop all the vegetables very finely and mix them together with seasoning **A**.
**3**  Heat 4 tblspns of the oil in a wok and stir-fry the chopped ingredients for 1½ minutes. Remove from the oil with a slotted spoon.
**4**  Divide the stuffing between the mushrooms pressing it into them firmly. Wash the beans and cook in boiling water for 2-3 minutes. Press one into the top of each stuffed mushroom.
**5**  Pour the oil from the wok into a large frying-pan. Put the mushrooms into the pan, stuffing side down in a single layer. Fry for a few minutes, then turn over carefully. Add seasoning **B**, bring to simmering point and simmer, covered, for 1 minute. Serve.

# 红乳燴豆腐

## Bean Curds in Red Fermented Sauce

### INGREDIENTS (SERVES 4)

2 bean curds
1 tspn salt
5 tblspns corn oil
1 red fermented bean curd
½ tblspn red juice from the
    fermented bean curd
1½ tblspns sugar

### SEASONING
50-75 ml/2-3 fl oz water
½ tspn white pepper
2 tspns sesame oil

### METHOD

**1**  Blanch bean curds in boiling water with the salt for 3 minutes. Drain and chop into dice.
**2**  Heat the oil in a wok. Mix the fermented bean curd with the red juice and the sugar, add to the wok and stir-fry over a medium heat, mashing the bean curd as you stir. Add the diced bean curds and the seasoning and stir everything together. Put the lid on the wok, and simmer until most of the liquid has been absorbed. Stir occasionally.

### NOTE
If you prefer, you can use cheese instead of the fermented bean curd. Any type of fermented bean curd can be used in this recipe; it does not have to be the red variety.

# 醬爆青菽

## Stir-fried Green Peppers with Bean Sauce

### INGREDIENTS (SERVES 4)

4 green peppers
4 tblspns corn oil
1 tblspn cornflour mixed with
    2 tblspns water

### SEASONING A
½ tblspn finely chopped
    spring onion
½ tblspn crushed garlic

### SEASONING B
2 tblspns hot bean sauce
1 tspn finely chopped red
    chilli
½ tblspn sugar
1 tblspn dark soy sauce
5 tblspns clear soup stock
    (see p. 116)

### METHOD

**1**  Wash the green peppers. Discard the stalk and seeds, then chop into 2.5-cm/1-inch sections.
**2**  Heat the oil in a wok and stir-fry seasoning **A** until lightly coloured. Add seasoning **B** and stir-fry for 1-2 minutes.
**3**  Add the green peppers to the wok and stir-fry over a high heat for 1 minute. Pour in the cornflour mixture and stir until the sauce thickens. Serve at once.

### NOTE
Add other vegetables such as shredded fungus, bamboo shoots and spiced bean curds to add variety, but do not use too many ingredients or you will spoil the clear taste of the dish.

## 玉米筍湯

# Baby Corn Shoot Soup

**INGREDIENTS** (SERVES 4)

6 Chinese mushrooms
12 baby corn shoots
3 salted bamboo shoots
4 tblspns green beans
600 ml/1 pint clear soup
    stock (see p. 116)
½ tspn salt
1 tspn sesame oil

**METHOD**

**1**   Soak the Chinese mushrooms in boiling water for 20 minutes. Drain. Cut off and discard the stalks and chop each cap in half.
**2**   Wash the baby corn shoots and chop them in half. Rinse the salted bamboo shoots under cold water and chop off the stalks and end parts. Wash again and chop into square sections. Wash the green beans.
**3**   Put all ingredients into a large bowl. Add the soup stock and salt and place the bowl in a steamer. Steam over boiling water for 20 minutes. Drizzle the sesame oil over the soup before serving.

**NOTE**
Salted bamboo shoots can be bought at Chinese supermarkets but you could substitute 50 g/2 oz of any salted vegetable for them.

## 韭菜干絲

# Stir-fried Dried Bean Curd Shreds with Chives

**INGREDIENTS** (SERVES 4)

50 g/2 oz chives
150 g/5 oz dried bean curd
   shreds or fresh egg noodles
4 tblspns corn oil
50-75 ml/2-3 fl oz clear soup
   stock (see p. 116)

**SEASONING**
1 tspn salt
1½ tspns sugar
½ tblspn light soy sauce
½ tspn white pepper

**METHOD**

**1**   Discard any old or withered leaves from the chives. Wash the remainder and chop into 4-cm/1½-inch sections. Chop the dried bean curd shreds into 2.5-cm/1-inch sections and wash in salted water.
**2**   Heat the oil in a wok. Add the soup stock with the dried bean curd shreds or noodles and the seasoning. Stir-fry over a gentle heat for 5-7 minutes, until the liquid has been absorbed. Add the chives and stir-fry for 30 seconds. Serve at once.

**NOTE**
A Chinese proverb runs "Chive is the chicken of the poor" and herbalists endorse that it is a very nutritious vegetable. It is easy to grow; do not neglect it.

# 金鈎掛玉牌

## Golden Hooks with Jade Plates

**INGREDIENTS** (SERVES 4)

225 g/8 oz yellow bean
    sprouts
2 cakes bean curd
2.5 × 4-cm/1 × 1½-in slice
    fresh root ginger, peeled
600 ml/1-pint clear soup
    stock (see p. 116)

**SEASONING**
1½ tspns salt
½ tspn white pepper

**METHOD**

**1**   Cut off and discard the end parts of the bean
sprouts. Wash the remainder and the bean curd.
**2**   Crush the ginger slightly with the edge of the
chopper; this makes it easier to peel and also releases
the juices.
**3**   Put all the ingredients except for the seasoning
into a pan and bring to the boil over medium heat.
Lower the heat and simmer for 30 minutes. Remove
the ginger, add the seasoning and serve.

**NOTES**
**1**   This is a delicately flavoured dish that is
particularly refreshing in the summer.
**2**   The recipe is so-called because yellow bean
sprouts look like golden hooks and the bean curds like
jade plates – to the imaginative!

# 豉汁蒸白蔣

## Steamed Water Chestnuts with Black Bean Sauce

**INGREDIENTS** (SERVES 4)

250 g/12 oz water chestnuts
150 ml/5 fl oz corn oil
2 tblspns black fermented
    beans
½ tblspn crushed garlic
3 tblspns green beans

**SEASONING**
½ tspn salt
½ tspn sugar
1 tspn white pepper

**METHOD**

**1**   Peel the water chestnuts and wash them. Fry in
hot oil for 2 minutes. Remove with a slotted spoon
and drain off the oil, reserving 1 tblspn in the pan.
**2**   Stir-fry the fermented beans and garlic until the
garlic has browned. Wash the green beans and add
them to the pan, stir-frying them for 1 minute.
**3**   Mix the stir-fried ingredients with the water
chestnuts in a bowl. Place this in a steamer and
steam over boiling water for 15-20 minutes. Add the
seasoning and serve.

**NOTE**
Fermented beans have a salty taste, whilst water
chestnuts are quite sweet. Season this dish carefully,
therefore, tasting it to make sure it is to your liking.

苦 海 慈 航

# Stuffed Bitter Gourds

## INGREDIENTS (SERVES 4)

6 Chinese mushrooms
1 bitter gourd
1 tblspn cornflour
3 tblspns green beans
100 g/4 oz water chestnuts
8 pieces spiced bean curds
6 tblspns corn oil

### SEASONING A

½ tspn salt
1 tblspn cornflour
½ tblspn sesame oil
⅓ tspn five-spice powder
½ tspn sugar

### SEASONING B

1½ tblspns light soy sauce
3 tblspns clear soup stock
   (see p. 116)
½ tblspn crushed garlic
1 tblspn black fermented
   beans
1 tblspn sugar
½ tspn salt

## METHOD

**1**   Soak the Chinese mushrooms in boiling water for 20 minutes. Drain. Cut off and discard the stalks.
**2**   Cut off and discard the stalk and top part from the bitter gourd, then chop it into sections. Scoop out the seeds and put the rings into a large pan of water. Bring to the boil and boil for 2 minutes. Drain and spread cornflour round the insides. Put on a plate.
**3**   Wash the green beans and cook them for 5 minutes in boiling water. Drain and cover with cold water.
**4**   Peel the water chestnuts and chop them finely with the spiced bean curds and the Chinese mushrooms caps. Mix in seasoning **A**.
**5**   Heat 4 tblspns oil in a wok and stir-fry the chopped ingredients for 1½ minutes. Remove from the wok with a slotted spoon and press into the bitter gourd rings. Put the plate into a steamer and steam over boiling water for 25 minutes.
**6**   Heat the remaining 2 tblspns oil in a wok. Drain the green beans and stir-fry with seasoning **B** for 30 seconds. Spoon over the bitter gourds and serve.

## NOTE

If you like, you could put the steamed bitter gourd into hot clear soup stock and serve this as a soup dish.

# 清炒節瓜

## Stir-Fried Fuzzy Melons

### INGREDIENTS (SERVES 4)

2 large or 4 small fuzzy
   melons
5 tblspns corn oil
1 tblspn ginger juice
1 tblspn water
1 tspn salt
green stems of 2 spring
   onions
2 tspns sherry

### METHOD

**1**   Peel the fuzzy melons and chop into slices.
**2**   Heat 4 tblspns oil in a wok and add the ginger
juice. Fry for 1 minute, then add the melon slices. Stir
for 1 minute more, then add the water and salt and
simmer over a medium heat, covered, for 3 minutes.
Stir from time to time. Transfer to a serving dish.
**3**   Chop the spring onion stems and stir-fry them
briefly in the remaining 1 tblspn oil. Sprinkle over the
fuzzy melons, add the sherry and serve.

### NOTE
Ginger juice is a flavouring agent and also a
tenderizer. It is made from fresh ginger. If you cannot
buy it, grate some fresh ginger and press it through a
sieve to extract the juice.

# 小家碧玉

## Stir-Fried Angled Luffa

### INGREDIENTS (SERVES 4)

2 angled luffas
4 tblspns corn oil
1 tblspn cornflour mixed with
   2 tblspns water
1½ tspns sesame oil

### SEASONING A
½ tblspn finely chopped
   spring onions
½ tspn crushed garlic

### SEASONING B
1 tspn salt
2 tblspns water

### METHOD

**1**   Peel the angled luffas. Wash them and chop into
triangular pieces.
**2**   Heat the oil in a wok and stir-fry seasoning **A** until
lightly coloured. Add the luffa together with
seasoning **B**, stir, then simmer for 1½ minutes,
stirring from time to time.
**3**   Add the cornflour paste, stirring until the mixture
thickens. Just before serving, stir in the sesame oil.

### NOTE
To make this dish more filling, you can add 1 piece of
dried bean curd sheet and 50g/2 oz fungus as shown
in the top small picture (right). Soak both these
ingredients for 1 hour in cold water, then shred and
stir-fry them for 3-4 minutes before adding the angled
luffa.

蠔油菜心燴鮑魚菇

# Abalone Mushrooms and Green Vegetables in Oyster Sauce

## INGREDIENTS (SERVES 4)

3-4 green-stemmed flat
   cabbages
275 g/10 oz abalone
   mushrooms
4 tblspns corn oil
125 ml/4 fl oz clear soup
   stock (see p. 116)
1 tblspn cornflour mixed with
   1½ tblspns water
½ tspn sesame oil

## SEASONING

1 tspn salt
1 tblspn oyster sauce
1½ tblspns sugar

## METHOD

**1**   Cut off and discard the root and any withered leaves from the cabbages. Wash them and cut in half.
**2**   Cut off and discard the stalks from the mushrooms. Wash and slice into large pieces.
**3**   Blanch the cabbage and mushrooms separately in boiling, salted water for 1 minute. Drain and plunge into cold water. Leave to cool, then drain again.
**4**   Heat the oil in a wok and stir-fry the cabbage and mushrooms. Add the seasoning, then the soup stock. Bring to the boil.
**5**   Stir in the cornflour mixture to thicken the sauce. Just before serving, stir in the sesame oil.

## NOTES

**1**   Plunging the cabbage and mushrooms into cold water after blanching helps to preserve their colour.
**2**   Substitute 225 g/8 oz straw mushrooms for the abalone mushrooms.

三鮮豆苗

# Stir-fried Spinach with Fresh Vegetables

## INGREDIENTS (SERVES 4)

450 g/1 lb spinach
6 straw mushrooms
1 carrot
1 bamboo shoot
5 tblspns corn oil
1 tspn cornflour mixed with 2 tspns water

### SEASONING
1 tspn salt
½ tspn white pepper

## METHOD

**1**  Discard the stalks and any old leaves from the spinach. Wash it well and shake off the water.
**2**  Wash the straw mushrooms and chop in half. Peel the carrot; slice it and the bamboo shoot.
**3**  Heat the oil in a wok and stir-fry the mushrooms, carrot and bamboo shoot for 3 minutes. Add the spinach and seasoning and stir-fry for 30 seconds more. Stir in the cornflour mixture to thicken the dish and serve at once.

## NOTE
The spinach most usually used in this dish is also called pea shoots. It can be stir-fried on its own as a nourishing vegetable. If you cannot get pea shoots, use ordinary spinach.

佛手飄香

# Chayotoes with Red Chilli Peppers

## INGREDIENTS (SERVES 4)

2 small chayotoes
3-4 red chillis
4 tblspns corn oil
4 tblspns water
1 tspn sherry

### SEASONING
1 tspn salt
½ tspn white pepper

## METHOD

**1**  Peel the chayotoes, then carefully cut away the white tissues. Cut in half and remove the seeds. Wash and slice.
**2**  Wash the red chillis and chop into fine slices.
**3**  Heat the oil in a wok and stir-fry the chillis until beginning to brown. Add the chayoto slices with the seasoning. Stir and add the water. Simmer, covered, for 1½ minutes.
**4**  Stir the ingredients, add the sherry and serve.

## NOTE
If chayoto is unavailable, substitute 4-5 small courgettes.

# 栗子燒香菇

# Braised Chestnuts with Chinese Mushrooms

**INGREDIENTS** (SERVES 4)

150 g/5 oz dried chestnuts
50 g/2 oz Chinese
   mushrooms
2 tspns sesame oil

**SEASONING**
3 tblspns dark soy sauce
1 tblspn rock sugar
⅓ tspn salt
7-8 slices liquorice

**METHOD**

**1**   Soak the dried chestnuts in cold water for at least 4 hours – the longer they are soaked, the quicker they cook and the more flavour they have. Drain and remove the red membrane. Wash them under cold running water.
**2**   Soak the Chinese mushrooms in boiling water for 20 minutes. Drain, reserving the soaking liquid. Cut off and discard the stalks.
**3**   Put about 300 ml/½ pint of the water used to soak the Chinese mushrooms in a saucepan and add the chestnuts, mushrooms and seasoning. Bring to the boil, then lower the heat and simmer for about 30 minutes until nearly all the liquid has been absorbed and the chestnuts are tender. Check the pan during cooking and add more water if necessary. Serve at once.

**NOTE**
Substitute peppermint leaves for liquorice.

# 釀茄夾

# Stuffed Aubergine Folders

**INGREDIENTS** (SERVES 4)

½ tblspn black moss
2 cakes bean curds
4 long aubergines
100 g/4 oz wheat flour
½ tspn salt
2 eggs
1 tblspn corn oil
water (see recipe)
1 pan of corn oil for deep
   frying

**SEASONING A**
½ tspn salt
½ tspn white pepper
1 egg white

**SEASONING B**
3 tblspns oyster sauce
1½ tblspns water
½ tspn salt
1 tblspn finely chopped
   spring onion
½ tblspn crushed garlic
2 tblspns corn oil

**METHOD**

**1**   Soak the black moss in cold water for 20 minutes.
**2**   Blanch the bean curds in boiling water for 3 minutes. Drain, cut off the hard edge and mash the remainder. Squeeze out any excess water.
**3**   Drain the black moss and mix with the mashed bean curd and seasoning **A**.
**4**   Wash the aubergines and discard the stem and top part. Chop into 15-mm/½-inch slices, then cut almost through these to make the 'folders'. Press about ½ tblspn of the bean curd mixture into each of these.
**5**   Mix the flour with the salt in a bowl. Make a well in the centre and tip in the eggs beaten with the tblspn corn oil. Gradually stir the flour into the eggs, adding sufficient water to make a smooth batter, the consistency of thick cream. Leave to stand for 10 minutes.
**6**   Mix together all the ingredients from seasoning **B** except for the oil. Heat the oil in a wok and stir-fry the ingredients for 2-3 minutes. Serve this as a sauce.
**7**   Dip the aubergine folders into the batter to coat them and fry them in the pan of deep oil for about 4 minutes each, until puffed up and golden. Drain on absorbent paper and serve with the sauce.

# Stir-Fried Mixed Vegetables

**INGREDIENTS** (SERVES 4)

5 bean curd sheets
450 g/1 lb watercress
4 triangular-shaped fried
   bean curds
3-4 small red chillis (optional)
4 tblspns corn oil
½ tblspn finely chopped
   spring onion
3 tblspns clear soup stock
   (see p. 116)
1½ tblspns cornflour mixed
   with 2 tblspns water

**SEASONING**
1 tspn salt
½ tspn sugar

**METHOD**

**1**   Soak the bean curd sheets in cold water for about 20 minutes to soften them. Drain.
**2**   Discard all old or withered leaves from the watercress keeping only the tender, fresh leaves. Wash them thoroughly and drain. Chop into 2.5-cm/ 1-inch sections.
**3**   Slice the fried bean curds and chop the bean curd sheets into big pieces. Chop the chillis, if using.
**4**   Heat the oil in a wok and stir-fry the shallots and chillis for 3-4 minutes. Add the watercress, fried bean curds, bean curd sheets, soup stock and seasoning. Cook, stirring for 3 minutes, then add the cornflour mixture and stir until the sauce has thickened. Serve at once.

**NOTE**
Old leaves and stalks from the watercress can be used to make soup. It is a very nutritious vegetable, said to be good for the lungs.

# Broad Beans with Mustard Sauce

**INGREDIENTS** (SERVES 4)

275 g/10 oz shelled broad
   beans
2 tblspns finely chopped
   spring onion

**SEASONING**
½ tspn salt
2 tblspns English mustard
½ tblspn sesame oil

**METHOD**

**1**   Wash the broad beans but do not peel off the skins. Cook for 5-8 minutes in simmering water until tender. Drain.
**2**   Mix the chopped spring onion with the seasoning and stir into the broad beans. Serve at once.

**NOTE**
The beans should be quite well cooked for this dish, but not so over-cooked that they turn mushy when you mix them with the other ingredients.

# Steamed Spiced Bean Curd with Green Beans

**INGREDIENTS** (SERVES 4)

4 cakes bean curd
50 g/2 oz green beans or
   salted vegetable
1 tblspn sesame oil

**SEASONING**
1½ tblspns light soy sauce
½ tspn salt
1 tspn sugar
½ tspn chilli powder

**METHOD**

**1**  Wash the bean curd and drain well. Dice.
**2**  Rub away the outer skin from the beans and blend them with the seasoning.
**3**  Put the diced bean curd on a plate and spoon the green beans on top. Steam over simmering water for 5-7 minutes. Stir in the sesame oil just before serving.

**NOTE**
If you use salted vegetable instead of green beans, it should be washed thoroughly and then chopped. Stir-fry the vegetable for 3 minutes before mixing with the seasoning.

# Stir-Fried Fungus with Lettuce and Pineapple

**INGREDIENTS** (SERVES 4)

225 g/8 oz fungus
1 head lettuce
50 g/2 oz pineapple slices,
   drained if canned
4 tblspns corn oil
1 tblspn cornflour mixed with
   2 tblspns water

**SEASONING**
1 tspn salt
½ tblspn sugar

**METHOD**

**1**  Chop off and discard the fungus roots. Wash the fungus, then soak in cold water for 1 hour until softened. Chop into pieces.
**2**  Peel the head lettuce, wash it and chop into slices.
**3**  Heat the oil in a wok and stir-fry all the ingredients, except the cornflour. Add the seasoning. Stir in the cornflour mixture and cook, stirring, until the mixture has thickened slightly. Remove and serve at once.

**NOTES**
**1**  This is a delicious tasting sweet and sour dish.
**2**  Substitute 100 g/4 oz straw mushrooms for the fungus, and 3 celery stalks for the head lettuce.

# 菇香菜粳
# Broth of Mushrooms and Cabbage

## INGREDIENTS (SERVES 4)

5-6 Chinese mushrooms
1 small cabbage
100 g/4 oz long-stem
   mushrooms
1 tblspn shredded preserved
   vegetable
4 tblspns corn oil
1 tblspn finely chopped
   spring onion
900 ml/1½ pints clear soup
   stock (see p. 116)
2 tblspns cornflour mixed
   with 2½ tblspns water

## SEASONING

1⅓ tspns salt
1 tspn sugar
⅔ tspn white pepper

## METHOD

**1**  Soak the Chinese mushrooms in boiling water for 20 minutes. Drain. Cut off and discard the stalks and shred the caps.
**2**  Cut off and discard the root and any withered leaves from the cabbage. Shred the remainder and wash. Cut off and discard the muddy roots from the long-stem mushrooms and wash clean. Wash the shredded preserved vegetables.
**3**  Heat the oil in a wok and stir-fry the Chinese mushroom and the spring onion for 2 minutes. Add the shredded cabbage and the seasoning and stir for 1 minute. Add the stock, bring to the boil, lower the heat and simmer, covered until the cabbage is tender – about 10 minutes. Add the long-stem mushrooms and cook, stirring, for 1 minute more.
**4**  Stir in the cornflour mixture and cook until the mixture thickens. Wash the shredded preserved vegetable and sprinkle this over the surface of the broth. Serve.


# 永结同心
# Black Moss with Vegetables and Dried Bean Curd Knots

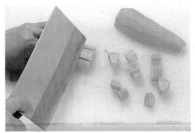

## INGREDIENTS (SERVES 4)

1 tblspn black moss
1 carrot
4 tblspns corn oil
1 tblspn finely chopped
   spring onion
100 g/4 oz dried bean curd
   knots (see NOTES)
¼ tspn bicarbonate of soda
150 ml/¼ pint clear soup
   stock (see p. 116)
10 straw mushrooms
1 tblspn cornflour mixed with
   2 tblspns water

## SEASONING

1 tspn salt
1 tspn sugar
½ tspn white pepper

## METHOD

**1**  Soak the black moss in water for 10 minutes. Drain. Peel the carrot and dice.
**2**  Heat the oil in a wok and stir-fry the spring onion until beginning to brown. Add the bean curd knots, bicarbonate of soda and the soup stock and bring to the boil. Boil for 3 minutes.
**3**  Add the seasoning, straw mushrooms, drained black moss and diced carrot and cook for 2 minutes more. Stir in the cornflour mixture and cook until the sauce thickens. Serve at once.

## NOTES

**1**  To make bean curd knots, soak bean curd sheets in cold water until soft. Pat dry in a clean cloth and cut into 10 × 2.5-cm/4 × 1-inch strips. Tie into knots and drop back into cold water for 5 minutes more, (see small picture 3, right).
**2**  Add 1 sliced, large white turnip to make the dish more substantial.

燒素肉饼

# Mixed Vegetable Patties

## INGREDIENTS (SERVES 4)

4 tblspns fungus
2-3 tblspns dried lily
4 tblspns shredded preserved
    vegetable
1 small onion
100 g/4 oz water chestnuts
1 bean curd
1 tblspn finely chopped
    spring onion
11 tblspns corn oil

### SEASONING A
4 tblspns cornflour
½ tspn salt
½ tspn white pepper

### SEASONING B
1½ tblspns light soy sauce
3 tblspns clear soup stock
    (see p. 116)
½ tblspn sugar

## METHOD

**1**   Soak the fungus in cold water for 1 hour until softened. Shred finely. Soak the dried lily in cold water for 30 minutes. Chop roughly. Wash the preserved vegetable.
**2**   Peel the onion and chop off the ends. Finely chop the remainder. Peel the water chestnuts and chop finely.
**3**   Blanch the bean curd in boiling water for 3 minutes. Drain well and mash with seasoning **A** and all the other ingredients except for the spring onion and the corn oil.
**4**   Heat 4 tblspns oil in a wok and stir-fry the mixture for 2 minutes. Remove and leave to go cold. Form into round cakes about 4 cm/1½ inches in diameter and 8 mm/¼ inch thick.
**5**   Heat 6 tblspns oil in a frying pan and fry the patties until golden brown on both sides. Arrange on a plate and sprinkle with the chopped spring onion.
**6**   Heat the remaining tblspn oil in a clean pan and add seasoning **B**. Bring to the boil, pour over the patties and serve.

煎茄絲餅

# Aubergine Patties

## INGREDIENTS (SERVES 4)

3 long aubergines
5 tblspns cornflour
75 ml/3 fl oz corn oil

### SEASONING A
⅓ tspn white pepper
½ tspn chilli powder
½ tspn salt
½ tblspn finely chopped
    spring onion

### SEASONING B
1 tblspn brown vinegar
1 tblspn light soy sauce
1 tblspn clear soup stock
    (see p. 116)
1 tblspn crushed garlic
½ tblspn sesame oil

## METHOD

**1**   Peel the aubergine and chop roughly. Soak in cold water for 15 minutes, then drain and steam for 7-8 minutes. Drain off any liquid and blend the aubergines with seasoning **A**. Leave to cool.
**2**   Stir the cornflour into the cooled aubergine, mixing them together thoroughly.
**3**   Heat a third of the oil in a frying pan over a medium heat. Drop in tblspns of the aubergine mixture and fry until golden brown on one side. Turn over and press the pattie flat with a fish slice. Fry until golden brown on this side. Keep adding oil to the pan as necessary until all the mixture has been cooked. Serve with seasoning **B**, mixed well together.

## NOTE
Sliced cucumber and tomato makes a tasty accompaniment to this dish. If you cannot find the long aubergines shown in small picutre 1, right, ordinary aubergines are perfectly suitable.

圍圍春濃

# Cream of Green Peas

### INGREDIENTS (SERVES 4)

1 × 410g/14 oz can green
 peas, drained
1 tomato
8 button mushrooms
6 tblspns corn kernels
250 ml/8 fl oz clear soup
 stock (see p. 116)
250 ml/8 fl oz milk
2½ tblspns cornflour
1½ tblspns single cream
2-3 grains orange comfit

### SEASONING
1½ tspns salt
⅓ tspn white pepper

### METHOD

**1**  Purée the drained peas. Wash the tomato and
chop. Wash the button mushrooms and dice. Wash
the corn kernels.
**2**  Mix these ingredients with the drained green peas
and the soup stock in a saucepan. Bring to the boil
over a medium heat and simmer for a few minutes,
stirring. Stir in the milk and the seasoning.
**3**  Mix the cornflour with the cream and stir into the
pea mixture. Simmer for 3 minutes, stirring all the
time to keep the mixture thick and creamy.
**4**  Chop the orange comfit and sprinkle it over the
soup.

### NOTE
Substitute 25 g/1 oz chopped almonds for the orange
comfit.

# Pineapple Cup

## INGREDIENTS (SERVES 4)

1 large fresh pineapple
100 g/4 oz gluten puff
75 g/3 oz baby corn shoots
50 g/2 oz water chestnuts
50 g/2 oz green beans
75 g/3 oz taro
1 tblspn corn oil
600 ml/1 pint clear soup
   stock (see p. 116)

## SEASONING

1½ tspns salt
½ tblspn sugar
½ tspn white pepper

## METHOD

**1** Scrub the pineapple and cut off the top part to make a lid. Scoop out the pulp, taking care not to pierce through the skin. Place the pineapple container in a large pan of water and bring to the boil. Simmer for 3 minutes, then remove the pineapple and rinse it under cold water.
**2** Soak the gluten puff in cold water for 20 minutes. Chop roughly.
**3** Wash the baby corn shoots and chop in half. Peel the water chestnuts and wash them together with the green beans. Chop taro into pieces and stir-fry in the oil for 3-4 minutes.
**4** Put the gluten puff, corn, water chestnuts, green beans, fried taro, soup stock and seasoning into the pineapple cup. Place in a dish and put this into a steamer. Steam over boiling water for 30 minutes. Serve at once.

## NOTES

**1** This has a delicious sweet and sour taste. Serve it with the pineapple leaves replaced as a lid.
**2** Look for a large pineapple that is still a little hard rather than a very ripe one. Reduce the amount of ingredients if they will not all fit in to the pineapple. Scalding the pineapple removes its rather sour taste which would spoil the delicate flavour of the dish.

# 四色沙拉

## Salad of Four Colours

### INGREDIENTS (SERVES 4)

2 cucumbers
150 g/5 oz broad beans
½ a small pumpkin
1 large potato
⅓ tspn white pepper
50 ml/2 fl oz yoghurt dressing
   (see NOTE)

### METHOD

**1**  Wash the cucumbers and cut off and discard the end parts. Cut in quarters lengthways and remove the seeds. Cut into chunks.
**2**  Wash the broad beans. Peel the pumpkin, cut into slices and remove the seeds. Wash the slices and cut into chunks. Peel the potato and wash, then cut into chunks, too.
**3**  Steam the broad beans, pumpkin and potato over gently boiling water for 15 minutes. Mix with the cucumber, pepper and dressing and serve.

### NOTE
To make yoghurt dressing, blend 50 ml/2 fl oz mayonnaise with 1 tblspn natural yoghurt, ¼ tspn caster sugar, a large pinch of salt and ½ tblspn each finely chopped onion and celery. Beat well for about 1 minute. Keep in the regrigerator in a strong polythene bag or a bowl cover with cling film until wanted.

---

# 奶汁蘆筍

## Asparagus with Milk

### INGREDIENTS (SERVES 4)

150 g/5 oz white asparagus
150 g/5 oz green asparagus
125 ml/4 fl oz milk
½ tblspn cornflour
3 tblspns single cream
2 tblspns finely shredded
   carrot

### SEASONING
1 tspn salt
½ tspn white pepper

### METHOD

**1**  Scrape away any old skin from the asparagus. Wash well and chop into 4-cm/1½-inch sections.
**2**  Blend the milk with the cornflour, keeping it smooth and free from lumps.
**3**  Blanch the asparagus in boiling water for 1½ minutes. Remove the green asparagus with tongs or a slotted spoon and leave the white asparagus for 1½ minutes more. Drain and put all the asparagus onto a plate.
**4**  Put the milk and cornflour into a small pan with the cream and the seasoning. Bring to the boil, stirring all the time, and when the mixture has thickened pour it over the asparagus. Serve at once with the shredded carrot.

### NOTES
**1**  Green asparagus will turn yellow if it is cooked for too long. A counsel of perfection would be to stand the asparagus upright so that the root part blanches for the full time, before turning them on their side so that the tips only blanch for 30 seconds.
**2**  If fresh asparagus is unobtainable, use canned asparagus.

# 滷塌棵菜

## Spiced Chinese Flat Cabbage

**INGREDIENTS** (SERVES 4)

450 g/1 lb Chinese flat
   cabbage
3 tblspns corn oil

**SEASONING**
½ tspn salt
½ tblspn sugar
2 tblspns dark soy sauce

**METHOD**

**1**   Cut off and discard any old or withered leaves
from the cabbage. Cut each one into 4 parts and wash
these thoroughly.
**2**   Heat the oil in a wok and stir-fry the cabbage with
the seasoning over a high heat for 1 minute. Put the
lid on the wok and simmer for 1 minute more. Stir the
cabbage and serve.

**NOTE**
If you prefer a thicker sauce, mix a little cornflour and
water into the cabbage.

# 酸辣洋葱

## Hot and Sour Onions

**INGREDIENTS** (SERVES 4)

2 onions
2-3 red chillis
4 tblspns corn oil

**SEASONING**
1 tspn salt
½ tblspn sugar
1 tblspn white vinegar
½ tblspn brown vinegar
pinch of white pepper

**METHOD**

**1**   Peel the onions and cut off the ends. Cut the
onions in half and then into square pieces.
**2**   Wash the chillis and slice diagonally.
**3**   Heat the oil in a wok and stir-fry the chillis for 1
minute. Add the onions and seasoning and stir-fry
over a high heat for 2-4 minutes. The onions should
still be crunchy. Serve.

**NOTE**
If you like the taste of raw onion, fry it for no more
than 1 minute before serving.

# 核桃酪

## Sweet Walnut Soup

**INGREDIENTS** (SERVES 4)

50 g/2 oz large red dates
100 g/4 oz walnut halves
100 g/4 oz rice flour
½ tblspn rock sugar powder
900 ml/1½ pints water

**METHOD**

**1**  Wash the red dates, then soak them in cold water for 4 hours. Cut open and remove the seeds. Wrap the pieces in a square of muslin and rub together by tapping with the back of a knife to loosen the skins. Soak in water for 10 minutes more to remove the skins, then mash the dates.
**2**  Grind the walnut halves to a powder. Mix together with the dates, rice flour and rock sugar powder. Tip into a pan and gradually stir in the water. Bring to the boil, stirring over a medium heat and serve.

**NOTES**
**1**  Walnuts are very nutritious and said to be particularly good for the elderly.
**2**  If you cannot get hold of rock sugar powder, use crystal rock sugar and crush it with the back of the chopper.

# 芝麻糊

## Sesame Paste

**INGREDIENTS** (SERVES 2)

3 tblspns sesame powder
3 tblspns brown sugar
450 ml/¾ pint boiling water

**METHOD**

**1**  Blend the sesame powder with the sugar. Gradually add the boiling water, stirring to keep the mixture smooth. Serve at once.

**NOTES**
**1**  There are two kinds of sesame powder on the market. One is pure sesame powder, the other a mixture of sesame powder and rice powder or cornflour. If using the pure one, add 1 tblspn cornflour, stirring this in with the sugar.
**2**  This dish is traditionally served as a dessert.

# Congee of Green Beans

### INGREDIENTS (SERVES 4)

100 g/4 oz green beans
3 tblspns millet
900 ml/1½ pints water

### SEASONING
1 tspn salt
4 tblspns sugar

### METHOD

**1** Wash the green beans and millet. Drain well.
**2** Bring the water to the boil and add the beans and millet. Lower the heat and simmer until the mixture has thickened – about 1 hour. Stir in the seasoning and serve at once.

### NOTE
Green beans can be used to make a drink which is said to relieve hypertension. Wash a good handful and put into a thermos jug. Pour in boiling water, screw on the lid and leave for 15 minutes. Strain and drink the liquid.

# Soup of Lily Petals with Lotus Seeds

### INGREDIENTS (SERVES 4)

50 g/2 oz dried lily (or 75-
   100 g/3-4 oz fresh)
100-150 g/4-5 oz dried lotus
   seeds (or 275 g/10 oz fresh)
900 ml/1½ pints water
50 g/2 oz rock sugar powder

### METHOD

**1** Soak dried lily overnight, then wash under cold running water. (If using fresh, just wash.)
**2** Soak dried lotus seeds in cold water for 4 hours, then wash under cold running water. (If using fresh, just wash.)
**3** Pour the water into a saucepan. Add the drained lily and lotus seeds and the rock sugar powder. Bring to the boil, then lower the heat and simmer for 40 minutes. Serve at once.

### NOTE
Lily and lotus seeds both make cooling tonics that provide particularly refreshing summer drinks.

# 糖醋高麗

## Sweet and Sour Lettuce

**INGREDIENTS** (SERVES 4)

½ a crispy lettuce
4 tblspns corn oil
½ tblspn crushed garlic
½ tblspn chopped red chillis

**SEASONING**
3 tblspns sugar
4 tblspns brown vinegar
1½ tspns salt

**METHOD**

**1** Discard outer withered leaves of the lettuce. Tear the remainder into large pieces and wash.
**2** Heat the oil in a wok and stir-fry the garlic and chillis over a medium heat for about 1 minute. Raise the heat and add the lettuce. Cook for 3 minutes more, stirring all the time. Add the seasoning, stir to mix, then remove from the heat and serve.

# 涼拌四季豆

## Cold Blended String Beans

**INGREDIENTS** (SERVES 4)

450 g/1 lb string beans
1 tspn salt
1 tblspn grated fresh ginger
    root
3 tblspns sesame sauce
    (see NOTES)

**METHOD**

**1** Cut off and discard the ends and stringy pieces from the beans. Wash under cold running water. Put into a pan of boiling water with the salt and grated ginger; cook for 2½ minutes.
**2** Drain the beans and plunge them straight into a pan of iced water. Leave until cold. Drain well and blend with the sesame sauce.

**NOTES**
**1** To make sesame sauce, blend together 1½ tblspns raw sesame sauce, 2 tblspns light soy sauce, ½ tspn salt, 3 tblspns cold boiled water, 1 tspn sugar and 1 tblspn sesame oil. If making the sauce to go with noodles, add more water and salt.
**2** Plunging the cooked beans into cold water will help preserve their colour. Choose even-sized beans for this dish.

# Three Tastes of Turnips

## INGREDIENTS (SERVES 6)

450 g/1 lb turnips
450 g/1 lb carrots

### SEASONING A
1½ tblspns light soy sauce
½ tblspn sesame oil
½ tspn white pepper
½ tspn salt

### METHOD A

**1** Peel the turnips and the carrots. Wash and chop into large chunks.
**2** Cook in boiling water until just tender. Drain and mix with seasoning **A**. Serve.

## INGREDIENTS
450 g/1 lb green turnips

### SEASONING B
3 tblspns light soy sauce
½ tblspn sesame oil

### DRESSING
¾ tspn salt
1 tblspn sugar

### METHOD B

**1** Wash the turnips well, but do not peel them. Chop into big slices and slice these almost down to the root (see picture opposite), so they resemble a comb.
**2** Rub the slices with the dressing, stirring them with your hands constantly. After 20 minutes, rinse and squeeze out the juice. Mix with seasoning **B**; leave for 10 minutes, then serve.

## INGREDIENTS
450 g/l lb green turnips

### SEASONING C
1 tblspn sugar
2 tblspns white vinegar
½ tspn white pepper

### DRESSING
¾ tspn salt
1 tblspn sugar

### METHOD C

**1** Wash the turnips well and dry them, then shred finely.
**2** Sprinkle the dressing over the turnips and leave for 30 minutes, stirring frequently with your hand. Rinse, squeeze out the juice, blend with seasoning **C** and serve.

### NOTES
**1** The dish in Method **B** is also known as Marinated Turnip. As it contains sesame oil it must be eaten the same day, but if you omit this ingredient, you can keep the turnip in a screw-top jar for several days.
**2** The dish in Method **C** should be served as soon as it is prepared.
**3** Substitute white Giant Radishes for the Turnip. English Turnips can be used in place of the Green Turnips.

# 麻油麵線

## Egg Noodles with Sesame Oil

### INGREDIENTS (SERVES 2)

1 packet (bundle) fresh egg
noodles
3 tblspns sesame oil
2 eggs, beaten
1 tblspn finely chopped fresh
ginger
1 slice fresh ginger
350 ml/12 fl oz clear soup
stock (see p. 116)
1 tspn salt

### METHOD

**1** Wash the noodles very thoroughly.
**2** Heat the oil in a wok and stir-fry the eggs over a
medium heat. When set, remove the eggs and stir-fry
the chopped ginger and the slice of ginger for 1
minute or so. Remove the slice of ginger and put on
one side. Pour the soup into the pan and add the salt.
Bring to the boil and add the noodles and fried egg.
Bring to the boil again and serve at once with the
slice of ginger to garnish.

### NOTES

**1** This is a famous dish from the Fuchow style of
cooking.
**2** Fresh egg noodles are sold in bundles.

# 清湯銀耳

## Soup of White Fungus

### INGREDIENTS (SERVES 4)

25 g/1 oz white fungus
4½ tblspns rock sugar
900 ml/1½ pints clear soup
stock (see p. 116)
4 maraschino cherries, for
decoration

### METHOD

**1** Soak the white fungus in cold water for 4-6 hours.
Remove the root and any hard pieces and wash the
fungus until it is quite clean. Soak for a further 2 hours
in hot water to allow it to expand. Drain off the water.
**2** Put the fungus and rock sugar into a bowl with
the clear soup. Place in a pan of hot water and simmer
very gently for 45 minutes to 1 hour until the soup
becomes glutinous. Check the pan from time to time
to make sure it does not burn dry. Serve the soup in
individual bowls with a cherry in each one.

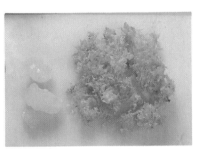

咖哩豆腐

# Curried Bean Curds

## INGREDIENTS (SERVES 4)

2 cakes bean curd
1½ tblspns finely chopped
   shallots
4 red or green chillis
4 tblspns corn oil
about 3 tblspns curry powder
50 ml/2 fl oz water
25 g/1 oz green beans
50 ml/2 fl oz milk
1 tblspn cornflour mixed with
   1½ tblspns water

### SEASONING
1½ tspns salt
1 tblspn sugar

## METHOD

**1**   Wash the bean curd and blanch in boiling water
for 3 minutes. Drain and cut into cubes.
**2**   Select the best parts of the shallots as you prepare
them. Wash the chillis and chop finely.
**3**   Heat the oil in a wok and stir-fry the chopped
shallot for 1 minute. Add the curry powder and fry for
about 30 seconds, stirring. Add the bean curd, chillis,
water and seasoning and cook for 3-5 minutes,
covered, but stirring frequently.
**4**   Meanwhile cook the green beans for 5 minutes in
boiling water. Drain.
**5**   Gradually stir the milk into the mixture in the wok,
then add the cornflour paste and cook, stirring until
the mixture thickens. Serve at once with the green
beans sprinkled on top.

### NOTE
This is a very hot dish; if you prefer a milder taste
reduce the amount of curry powder and replace the
chilli with chopped green pepper.

小 炒 四 季

# Stir-Fried String Beans

## INGREDIENTS (SERVES 4)

225 g/8 oz string or runner
   beans
4 tblspns corn oil
½ tblspn shredded red chillis
1 tblspn shredded fresh root
   ginger

### SEASONING
1 tspn salt
2 tspns light soy sauce
1 tspn sugar

## METHOD

**1**   Top and tail the beans. Wash them, then slice
diagonally.
**2**   Heat the oil in a wok and stir-fry the chillis and
ginger over a high heat for 30 seconds. Add the beans
and seasoning and stir-fry for 1½ minutes more. Serve
at once.

### NOTE
If you like, add I crushed garlic clove, stir-frying it
with the chillis.

# 撥魚麵湯
## Soup of Dough Slices

### INGREDIENTS (SERVES 4)

3 large Chinese mushrooms
150-225 g/5-8 oz wheat flour
½ tspn salt
1 egg
water (see recipe)
50 g/2 oz fungus
1 carrot
100 g/4 oz Chinese greens
900 ml/1½ pints clear soup
    stock (see p. 116)

### METHOD

**1** Soak the Chinese mushrooms in boiling water for 20 minutes. Drain. Cut off and discard the stalks and slice the caps.
**2** Mix the wheat flour with the salt, then beat in the egg and sufficient water to make a very thick batter. Leave it to stand for 20 minutes, then beat again thoroughly.
**3** Wash the fungus and slice it. Peel and slice the carrot and wash and shred the Chinese greens, using only the green parts.
**4** Put all the vegetables in a large pan with the soup stock. Bring to the boil, then add spoonfuls of the batter, keeping the soup boiling all the time. When you have added all the batter to the pan, simmer for 5 minutes more then serve.

### NOTE
For those who include fish in their diet, a few cooked, peeled prawns can be added to the soup

# 玉米湯
## Cream of Corn Soup

### INGREDIENTS

900 ml/1½ pints clear soup
    stock (see p. 116)
50 g/2 oz plain flour
450 g/1 lb corn kernels
1 carrot
4 tblspns green peas
1½ tspns salt
2 tblspns sugar
1 tspn black pepper
2 tblspns single cream
1 slice bread, toasted

### METHOD

**1** Put about a third of the soup stock into a saucepan and stir in the flour, keeping the mixture smooth.
**2** Liquidize the corn kernels with the rest of the soup stock and gradually stir this into the mixture in the pan, keeping it smooth and free from lumps.
**3** Peel the carrot and chop into cubes. Add to the soup with the peas, salt and sugar and simmer for 5 minutes. Just before serving, stir in the pepper and cream and sprinkle the toast, cut into cubes, over the surface.

芋　泥

# Taro Mash

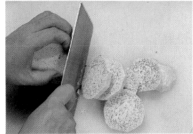

### INGREDIENTS (SERVES 4)

450 g/1 lb taro
450 ml/¾ pint rich soup stock
　(see p. 116)
3 tblspns single cream

### SEASONING

1½ tspns salt
½ tblspn sugar
½ tspns white pepper

### METHOD

**1**　Peel the taro and wash thoroughly. Chop into thick slices and steam over boiling water for 25 minutes until soft. Mash thoroughly.
**2**　Stir the soup stock into the mashed taro and add the seasoning. Rub through a sieve.
**3**　Put the taro purée into a pan and slowly bring to the boil. Stir in the cream and serve at once.

### NOTE

You can substitute vegetable oil for the cream. This dish is commonly served with fried noodles as a snack.

辣　炒　軟　絲

# Hot Bottle Gourd Shreds

### INGREDIENTS (SERVES 4)

1 bottle gourd
6 tblspns corn oil
2 tblspns shredded red chillis
1 tblspn finely chopped garlic
1 tblspn cornflour mixed with
　2 tblspns water

### SEASONING

1 tspn salt
1 tspn sugar

### METHOD

**1**　Peel the bottle gourd and wash it. Chop into slices, then shred these finely.
**2**　Heat the oil in a wok and stir-fry the chillis and garlic for 1 minute over a high heat. Add the shredded bottle gourd with the seasoning and stir-fry for a minute more.
**3**　Lower the heat and cook, stirring occasionally, until the gourd is tender. Stir in the cornflour paste and cook until the mixture has thickened. Serve at once.

### NOTE

Look for a bottle gourd that feels heavy and looks fresh around the stalk.

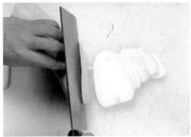

# Vegetable String Of Colours

## INGREDIENTS (SERVES 4)

6 large Chinese mushrooms
2 green peppers
12 water chestnuts
1 small yam
4 spiced bean curds
1 carrot
2 cucumbers

## SEASONING

1 tblspn crushed garlic
3 tblspns light soy sauce
1½ tblspns sugar
½ tspn salt
2 tblspns water
2 tblspns Hoisin sauce
1 tspn dry sherry

## METHOD

**1** Soak the Chinese mushrooms in boiling water for 20 minutes. Drain. Cut off and discard the stalks and cut the caps in half.
**2** Wash the green peppers, cut in half and discard the seeds and stalk part. Chop into chunks. Wash the water chestnuts. Peel the yam, wash and slice.
**3** Wash the spiced bean curds and chop into 8 triangular shapes. Peel the carrot, wash and slice. Wash the cucumbers, cut off the end parts and slice.
**4** Put the seasoning ingredients into a small pan and bring to the boil, stirring. Take off the heat.
**5** Thread the vegetables alternately onto bamboo sticks, brush with the seasoning and grill for about 5 minutes on each side. Brush continually with the seasoning during grilling.

## NOTE

An alternative method of cooking is to fry the skewered vegetables in corn oil for 3-5 minutes on either side. Serve them with the seasoning as a sauce.

# 烤素方

## Fried Vegetable Folds

### INGREDIENTS (SERVES 4)

12 dried bean curd sheets
3 eggs
4 tblspns finely chopped
    spring onion
1 tspn five-spice powder
½ tspn salt
1 tblspn light soy sauce
1 pan of vegetable oil for
    deep frying

### METHOD

**1**   Soak the bean curd sheets in cold water for 20-30 minutes to soften them. Pat dry with absorbent paper, taking care not to break or tear them.
**2**   Beat the eggs with the spring onions, five-spice powder, salt and the soy sauce.
**3**   Lay 1 of the bean curd sheets flat and brush with the beaten egg mixture. Place another sheet on top and brush with the egg mixture. Fold up as shown in the small picture 3. Repeat this brushing and folding process with the remainder of the bean curd sheets.
**4**   Cut the folded sheets into squares or triangles being very careful not to tear them.
**5**   Heat the oil and deep-fry the bean curd folds for 4-5 minutes. Remove with a slotted spoon and drain on absorbent paper before serving.

# 腐衣香菜

## Bean Curd Rolls with Basil

### INGREDIENTS (SERVES 4)

10 dried bean curd sheets
50 g/2 oz basil leaves
2 tblspns wheat flour mixed
    with 1½ tblspns water
1 pan of corn oil for deep
    frying

### SEASONING
1 tspn salt
2 tspns sugar
½ tspn white pepper

### METHOD

**1**   Soak the bean curd sheets in cold water for 20-30 minutes to soften them. Pat dry with absorbent paper, taking care not to break or tear them.
**2**   Pick off and discard any old or withered leaves from the basil, and wash the remainder. Dry, then chop with 4 of the bean curd sheets. Mix in the seasoning.
**3**   Lay 2 sheets of bean curd flat, one on top of the other. Put a third of the basil mixture on one end, then roll up the bean curd as shown in the small picture 2. Brush the end with the wheat flour paste to seal. Make 2 more rolls with the remaining 4 sheets of bean curd and the basil mixture.
**4**   Heat the oil and deep-fry the rolls for about 5 minutes. Remove and drain on absorbent paper and leave to cool. When cold cut into sections and serve.

### NOTES
**1**   You could substitute white wormwood, chives or bean sprouts for the basil.
**2**   If you prefer, serve the rolls hot, cutting them into sections as soon as they are cooked.

扑 双 冬

# Stir-Fried Bamboo Shoots with Chinese Mushrooms

**INGREDIENTS** (SERVES 4)

12 Chinese mushrooms
3 bamboo shoots
4 tblspns corn oil

**SEASONING**
⅔ tspn salt
2 tblspns soy sauce
½ tblspn sugar

**METHOD**

**1**   Soak the Chinese mushrooms in boiling water for 20 minutes. Drain, reserving 3 tblspns of the soaking water. Cut off and discard the stalks and cut the caps in half if they are very large.
**2**   Peel the bamboo shoots and cut in half. Cook in boiling water for 20 minutes, drain and plunge in cold water, leaving to cool completely. Drain and cut into 15-mm/½-inch thick slices.
**3**   Heat the oil in a wok and stir-fry the bamboo for 3 minutes. Add the Chinese mushrooms, seasoning and the reserved water from the Chinese mushrooms. Stir everything together, put the lid on the wok and simmer for 5 minutes. Serve.

炒 珍 珠 菜

# Stir-Fried White Wormwood

**INGREDIENTS** (SERVES 4)

450 g/1 lb white wormwood
4 tblspns corn oil

**SEASONING**
1 tspn salt

**METHOD**

**1**   Tear off and discard any old or withered leaves from the white wormwood. Wash and dry, then tear into sections.
**2**   Heat the oil in a wok and stir-fry the white wormwood with the seasoning for 1½ minutes. Serve at once.

**NOTE**
If white wormwood is unavailable, use Chinese cabbage or bean sprouts instead.

# Stir-Fried Chinese Red Spinach

**INGREDIENTS** (SERVES 4)

900 g/2 lbs Chinese red
  spinach
7 tblspns corn oil
2 tblspns chopped garlic
1 tblspn cornflour mixed with
  2 tblspns water

**SEASONING**
1 tspn salt
½ tspn white pepper
2 tspns sugar

**METHOD**

**1**  Tear off and discard any old or withered parts
from the spinach. Wash the remainder, rubbing it
together to clean it thoroughly.
**2**  Heat the oil in a wok and stir-fry the garlic for 1
minute. Add the spinach and seasoning and stir. Put
the lid on the wok and simmer the spinach until it is
well cooked and tender. Stir in the cornflour to
thicken and serve at once.

**NOTE**
Substitute 450 g/1 lb broccoli for the red spinach.

# Sponge Gourd Pan Sticks

**INGREDIENTS** (SERVES 4)

1 medium sponge gourd
50-75 ml/2-3 fl oz corn oil
1 tblspn chopped preserved
  vegetable (optional)
½ tspn salt
½ tblspn finely chopped
  spring onion
6 tblspns cornflour

**SEASONING**
2 tblspns light soy sauce
3 tblspns clear soup stock
  (see p. 116)
½ tblspn finely chopped red
  chillis
1 tblspn finely chopped garlic
3 tblspns sesame oil

**METHOD**

**1**  Peel the sponge gourd and cut off the stalk. Wash,
chop in half and slice thinly.
**2**  Heat 2 tblspns oil in a wok and stir-fry the gourd
slices and preserved vegetable (if used) for a few
minutes. Remove and mix with the salt and spring
onion. When cool, mix carefully with the cornflour.
**3**  Heat half the remaining oil in a frying pan and fry
tablespoonfuls of the gourd mixture, pressing flat
with a fish slice. Fry over a medium heat until brown
on both sides. Repeat until the mixture is finished,
adding more oil as necessary. Serve hot with the
seasoning ingredients mixed together, as a dip.

**NOTE**
Instead of the sauce suggested, serve with chilli
sauce or English mustard.

# 高風亮節

## Stir-Fried Baby Bamboo Shoots with Red Chilli

**INGREDIENTS** (SERVES 4)

450 g/1 lb baby bamboo
   shoots
4 red chillis
4 tblspns corn oil
½ tblspn crushed garlic
50 ml/2 fl oz clear soup stock
   (see p. 116)

**SEASONING**
1 tspn salt
1½ tblspns light soy sauce
1 tblspn sugar

**METHOD**

**1**  Tear off the old stalks and skins from the baby
bamboo shoots and wash. Wash the chillis and slice
finely.
**2**  Heat the oil in a wok and stir-fry the chillis and
garlic for 1 minute. Add the baby bamboo shoots and
the seasoning, and stir thoroughly. Pour in the soup
stock and simmer, covered, until most of the liquid
has been absorbed. Serve at once.

**NOTES**
**1**  Baby bamboo shoots are sweet and crispy.
**2**  If you would rather the dish is not too hot,
substitute red peppers for the chillis.

---

# 留芳百世

## Stir-Fried Taro Stalk with Peanuts

**INGREDIENTS** (SERVES 4)

450 g/1 lb taro stalks
6 tblspns peeled peanuts
5 tblspns corn oil
1 tblspn crushed garlic

**SEASONING**
1 tspn salt
1 tspn sugar
½ tblspn soy sauce

**METHOD**

**1**  Tear the taro stalks apart and peel away the
stringy skin. Chop off the end part, then wash the
stalks and chop into 2.5-cm/1-inch diagonal slices.
**2**  Put the peanuts in a strong polythene bag and
crush them with the back of the chopper.
**3**  Heat the oil in a wok and stir-fry the garlic for 1
minute. Add the taro slices and stir-fry for 3 minutes
more. Add the seasoning and the crushed peanuts,
and cook, covered for 3 minutes or until the taro is
tender. Stir once more and serve.

**NOTE**
Look for tender young taro stalks for this recipe and
be sure to cook them until they are quite soft. If they
are unavailable, use mange touts instead.

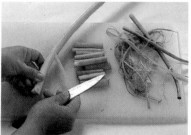

# 鳳尾生雲

## Clear Soup of Bamboo Shoots

### INGREDIENTS (SERVES 4)

150 g/5 oz pickled bamboo
shoots
900 ml/1½ pints clear soup
stock (see p. 116)

### SEASONING
·1½ tspns salt
½ tspn white pepper

### METHOD

**1**  Wash the pickled bamboo shoots and chop off the
ends. Tear the remainder of the shoots into long
shreds.
**2**  Bring the soup stock to the boil, add the bamboo
shoots and seasoning, bring back to the boil and
simmer for 3 minutes.

### NOTE
Use tender bamboo shoots for this dish. It is a
particularly refreshing soup for a summer evening.
The torn shreds of bamboo shoots resemble birds'
tails, which is how it gets its more romantic name of
Cloudbuilt Phoenix Tails.

# 菇香呈祥

## Golden Mushrooms in Ginger Juice

### INGREDIENTS (SERVES 4)

450 g/l lb button mushrooms
salt
125 ml/4 fl oz plus 2 extra
    tblspns corn oil
2 tblspns soy sauce
½ tblspn ginger juice
½ tblspn cornflour mixed
    with 1 tblspn water

### SEASONING

⅔ tspn salt
1 tblspn sugar
⅓ tspn white pepper

### METHOD

**1**  Wash the button mushrooms in water mixed with
a little salt. Dry on absorbent paper and make slanting
cuts round the caps.
**2**  Heat the 125 ml/4 fl oz of oil in a wok and stir-fry
the mushrooms until they have turned golden.
Remove with a slotted spoon and soak in the soy
sauce for 20 minutes.
**3**  Heat the remaining 2 tblspns oil in a clean pan
and stir-fry the ginger juice for ½ minute. Add the
mushrooms and the seasoning and stir-fry for a few
minutes. Add the cornflour paste, let the sauce
thicken and serve.

# Soup of Assorted Shreds

### INGREDIENTS (SERVES 4)

25 g/1 oz dried bean curd
  sheets
50 g/2 oz fungus
5-6 Chinese mushrooms
50 g/2 oz bamboo shoot
900 ml/1½ pints clear soup
  stock (see p. 116)

### SEASONING
1½ tspns salt
½ tspn white pepper

### METHOD

**1**  Soak the dried bean curd sheets and the fungus in cold water for about 20 minutes until softened. Drain and shred finely.
**2**  Soak the Chinese mushrooms in boiling water for 20 minutes. Drain. Cut off and discard the stalks and shred the caps finely.
**3**  Peel the bamboo shoot. Wash it and shred finely.
**4**  Put all the shredded ingredients into a bowl (see picture opposite). Add the seasoning and carefully pour in the soup stock, taking care not to disarrange the vegetables. Steam over gently boiling water for 40 minutes. Serve straight away.

# Bean Curd Rolls with Mushrooms

### INGREDIENTS (SERVES 4)

16 pieces of dried bean curd
  sheets
4 Chinese mushrooms
7 tblspns light soy sauce
2½ tblspns sugar
1 tspn five-spice powder
½ tspn salt
1 tblspn sesame oil
300 ml/½ pint clear soup
  stock (see p. 116)
1 tblspn rock sugar
8 pieces of liquorice or
  peppermint leaves
1 stick cinnamon

### METHOD

**1**  Soak the dried bean curd sheets in cold water for 20-30 minutes. Pat dry with absorbent paper, taking care not to tear the sheets.
**2**  Soak the Chinese mushrooms in boiling water for 20 minutes. Drain. Cut off and discard the stalks and finely chop the caps. Mix with 4 tblspns soy sauce, the sugar, five-spice powder, salt and sesame oil. Put in a small pan, bring to the boil and simmer for 1 minute.
**3**  In a separate pan, put the soup stock, the rest of the soy sauce, rock sugar, liquorice or peppermint leaves and the cinnamon. Bring to the boil, lower the heat and simmer for 20 minutes. Discard the cinnamon stick.
**4**  Lay a sheet of bean curd flat and brush with the Chinese mushroom mixture. Repeat, layering and brushing 8 bean curd sheets together. Roll up, then repeat with the remaining 8 sheets of bean curd.
**5**  Wrap the bean curd rolls in muslin and tie with strings to secure. Steam for 25 minutes. Remove, cool slightly, then discard the string and muslin. Serve in slices with the soup stock sauce.

73

# 木耳燒素肉

## Stir-Fried Glutens with Fungus

**INGREDIENTS** (SERVES 4)

225 g/8 oz gluten puff
2 tblspns light soy sauce
1 pan of corn oil for deep
    frying
50 g/2 oz fungus
small piece fresh root ginger
3 tblspns oil
3 tblspns clear soup stock
    (see p. 116)

**SEASONING**
1 tspn salt
1½ tblspns sugar
½ tspn white pepper

**METHOD**

**1**   Tear the gluten puff into pieces. Mix with the soy sauce and leave for 20 minutes.
**2**   Heat the oil and deep fry the gluten puff for 30 seconds. Remove with a slotted spoon and drain on absorbent paper.
**3**   Cut off and discard the roots from the fungus. Wash and slice.
**4**   Peel the ginger and cut in slices.
**5**   Heat the 3 tblspns oil in a wok and stir-fry the fungus and ginger. Add the fried gluten puff and the seasoning. Stir-fry for a minute, then add the soup stock and simmer, covered, for 1-2 minutes more. Serve at once.

**NOTE**
You could add shredded cucumber and carrot to this dish to give it a bit of colour.

# 糟香麵筋

## Marinated Glutens with Red Fermented Sauce

**INGREDIENTS** (SERVES 4)

225 g/8 oz gluten puff
1½ tblspns red fermented
    grain sauce or 2 red
    fermented bean curds
4 tblspns corn oil

**SEASONING**
1 tblspn sugar
3 tblspns clear soup stock
    (see p. 116)

**METHOD**

**1**   Wash the gluten puff and dry on absorbent paper. Cut into slanting pieces.
**2**   Blend the red fermented grain sauce or the fermented bean curds with the seasoning, mashing them together. Add the glutens and leave for 20 minutes.
**3**   Heat the oil in a wok and stir-fry the marinated glutens over a medium heat for 3 minutes. Serve at once.

**NOTE**
Any fermented bean curd sauce could be used instead of the red fermented grain sauce.

# Home-Town Style Mange Tout

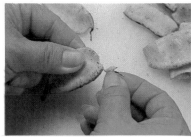

**INGREDIENTS** (SERVES 4)

350 g/12 oz mange tout
4 tblspns corn oil
½ tblspn finely chopped fresh
  root ginger
⅓ tblspn crushed garlic
⅓ tblspn finely chopped red
  chillis

**SEASONING**
1 tspn salt
½ tspn sherry

**METHOD**

**1**  Top and tail the mange tout, removing any stringy pieces. Wash.
**2**  Heat the oil in a wok and stir-fry the ginger, garlic and chillis for 1 minute. Add the mange tout and stir. Cook over a medium heat, covered, for 1 minute, then add the seasoning, and cook, stirring, for a further minute. Serve at once.

**NOTE**
Mange tout are also known as snow peas.

# Stir-Fried Chinese Cabbage with Chinese Mushrooms

**INGREDIENTS** (SERVES 4)

5 Chinese mushrooms
50 g/2 oz dried lily flowers
1 medium Chinese cabbage
4 tblspns corn oil
½ tblspn cornflour mixed
  with 2 tblspns water

**SEASONING**
1 tspn salt
½ tblspn sugar

**METHOD**

**1**  Soak the Chinese mushrooms in boiling water for 20 minutes. Drain. Cut off and discard the stalks and shred the caps.
**2**  Cut off and discard the hard stem parts from the dried lily flowers. Tie a knot in each of the flowers, wash them and soak in cold water for about 30 minutes. Drain and squeeze dry.
**3**  Cut off and discard the root part and any old or withered leaves from the cabbage. Wash the leaves and cut into wide shreds.
**4**  Heat the oil in a wok and stir-fry the mushroom shreds for 1-2 minutes. Add the cabbage and lily flowers and stir. Lower the heat, and cook covered, until the cabbage is soft.
**4**  Stir in the seasoning and the cornflour paste, and cook until the mixture has thickened. Serve at once.

# 福壽暖鍋
# *Pot of Assorted Vegetables*

**INGREDIENTS** (SERVES 4)

25 g/1 oz dried lily flowers
½ a small cabbage
1 carrot
1 turnip
½ a medium cauliflower
1 small taro
100 g/4 oz wheat flour
½ tspn salt
1 tspn chilli powder
4 eggs
50-75 ml/2-3 fl oz water
5 tblspns corn oil
3 tblspns shredded preserved
    vegetable
1.2 litres/2 pints clear soup
    stock (see p. 116)

**SEASONING**

1½ tspns salt

**METHOD**

**1**    Cut off and discard the hard stem parts from the dried lily flowers. Tie a knot in each of the flowers, wash them, then soak in cold water for about 30 minutes. Drain and squeeze dry.
**2**    Cut off and discard the root and any old or withered leaves from the cabbage. Wash the leaves and shred them.
**3**    Peel the carrot and turnip, wash and dice. Wash the cauliflower, cut off and discard any tough stalks and cut into small florets. Peel the taro and shred it.
**4**    Mix together the wheat flour, salt and chilli powder and mix to a smooth batter with the eggs, water and 1 tblspn oil. Coat the cauliflower, cabbage and taro with this batter.
**5**    Heat the remaining oil and fry the battered vegetables until golden brown. Remove and keep warm. Pour off all but 1 tblspn of the oil.
**6**    Stir fry the preserved vegetable in the oil for a few minutes, then add the seasoning, soup stock, carrot and turnip. Bring to the boil and simmer for 5 minutes. Stir in the dried lily flowers and the fried battered vegetables. Serve at once.

# 全福暖鍋
# *Family Pot*

**INGREDIENTS** (SERVES 4)

8 Chinese mushrooms
9 pieces of dried bean curd
    sheets
10 water chestnuts
2 tblspns corn oil
1 carrot
2 pieces of fried bean curd
    sheet
2-3 water bamboos
8 seaweed rolls
9 tblspns finely chopped
    preserved vegetable
2 tblspns shredded bamboo
    shoots
6 tblspns chopped fungus
12 pieces wonton skin
1 slice fresh root ginger
1.2 litres/2 pints clear soup
    stock (see p. 116)
50 g/2 oz bean sprouts

**SEASONING**

1½ tblspns salt
½ tblspn sugar
2 tblspns soy sauce
½ tspn white pepper

**METHOD**

**1**    Soak the Chinese mushrooms in boiling water for 20 minutes. Drain. Cut off and discard the stalks.
**2**    Soak the dried bean curd sheets in cold water for 20 minutes until soft. Drain and shred 1 of them finely.
**3**    Peel and wash the water chestnuts and fry them in the oil for 2 minutes. Remove with a slotted spoon.
**4**    Peel the carrot and chop into chunks. Divide the fried bean curd sheet into 4 pieces.
**5**    Discard the skins from the water bamboos and cut off the stalks. Chop into chunks and wash. Wash the seaweed rolls.
**6**    Mix 3 tblspns of chopped preserved vegetable with the shredded dried bean curd sheet and the bamboo shoots. Mix the dried bean curd sheets into this.
**7**    Mix the rest of the preserved vegetable with the fungus and wrap in the wonton skins.
**8**    Put the ginger and soup into a large saucepan and bring to the boil. Add the carrot, Chinese mushrooms, water bamboo, water chestnuts, seaweed rolls and the dried bean curd sheet mixture. Bring to the boil and simmer gently for 20 minutes. Add the seasoning, the wonton parcels and bean sprouts, and serve.

# 双菇扒芥菜

# Mustard Greens with Mushrooms

## INGREDIENTS (SERVES 4)

450 g/1 lb mustard greens
   (or a crisp lettuce)
100 g/4 oz straw mushrooms
100 g/4 oz button mushrooms
½ tspn bicarbonate of soda
4 tblspns corn oil
½ tblspn crushed garlic
1 tspn finely chopped fresh
   root ginger
75 ml/3 fl oz clear soup stock
   (see p. 116)
1 tblspn cornflour mixed with
   2 tblspns water
1 tspn sesame oil

### SEASONING

1 tspn salt
2 tspns sugar

## METHOD

**1**   Cut off and discard any withered or old parts from the mustard greens. Wash and chop into chunks.
**2**   Wash the straw mushrooms and the button mushrooms. Cut off and discard any muddy stalks and cut them all in half. Blanch in boiling water for 1 minute, drain (reserving the water) and plunge into cold water. Leave to cool.
**3**   Add the bicarbonate of soda to the boiling water used to blanch the mushrooms. Add the mustard greens and cook for 1½ minutes. Drain and rinse under cold running water.
**4**   Heat the oil in a wok and stir-fry the garlic and ginger for 1 minute. Add the mustard greens and half of the seasoning. Stir-fry for 1 minute, then remove with a slotted spoon.
**5**   Add the soup stock, and the straw and button mushrooms to the pan. Bring to the boil, stir in the rest of the seasoning and cook for 1 minute. Stir in the cornflour mixture, and when the sauce has thickened, pour it over the mustard greens. Dribble over the sesame oil and serve.

# 農 家 樂

# The Farmer's Joy

## INGREDIENTS (SERVES 4)

225 g/8 oz vermicelli
350 g/12 oz white Chinese
   cabbage
1 large fungus
1 large carrot
4 tblspns corn oil
1 tblspn chopped spring
   onion
50 ml/2 fl oz clear soup stock
   (see P. 116)

### SEASONING

⅔ tspn salt
1½ tblspns soy sauce
1 tspn sugar

## METHOD

**1**   Soak the vermicelli in cold water for 15 minutes until softened. Cut into sections.
**2**   Cut off and discard the root and any old or withered leaves from the Chinese cabbage. Wash and chop into 2.5-cm/1-inch slices. Wash the fungus and slice.
**3**   Peel the carrot and chop into large slices.
**4**   Heat the oil in a wok and stir-fry the spring onion for 1 minute. Add the fungus and carrot slices and stir-fry for 1 minute more. Add the white cabbage and cook, stirring, for a few minutes.
**5**   Add the drained vermicelli, the soup stock, and the seasoning, mixing everything together well. Bring to the boil, simmer, covered for 1 minute and serve.

### NOTE
Add bamboo shoot, Chinese mushrooms and bean curd sheets to this dish if you want to make it more substantial.

# 豆絲春濃

## Stir-Fried Bean Cake Shreds with String Beans

**INGREDIENTS** (SERVES 4)

150-175 g/5-6 oz green bean
  starch
75-100 g/3-4 oz rice flour
water (see recipe)
50 g/2 oz string beans
50 g/2 oz fungus
50 g/2 oz bean sprouts
5 tblspns corn oil
⅔ tspn chilli powder
25 ml/1 fl oz clear soup stock
  (see p. 116)

**SEASONING**
1 tspn salt
1 tblspn dark soy sauce

**METHOD**

**1** Blend the green bean starch and the rice flour
with sufficient water to make a pliable dough. Knead
it, then press it out thinly. Put it in a frying pan and
cook on both sides over a medium heat until
beginning to brown. Remove and chop into fine
shreds.
**2** Top and tail the beans, removing any stringy bits.
Chop into diagonal slices. Wash the fungus and
shred. Wash the bean sprouts.
**3** Heat the oil in a wok and fry the chilli powder for
30 seconds. Add the beans, fungus and bean sprouts
and stir-fry for 1 minute. Add the shredded cooked
dough and the soup stock and simmer, covered, for 1
minute. Serve at once.

# 脆味瓜片

## Pickled Cucumber Slices

**INGREDIENTS** (SERVES 4)

450 g/1 lb cucumbers
2 tblspns white vinegar
3 tblspns sesame oil

**SEASONING**
2½ tspns salt
4 tblspns sugar

**METHOD**

**1** Wash the cucumbers, cut off and discard end
parts and then slice finely.
**2** Mix the cucumber slices with the seasoning,
mixing them together well. Put in a dish and chill.
**3** Just before serving, squeeze out the excess liquid
from the cucumbers and blend with the vinegar and
sesame oil. Serve.

**NOTE**
You can keep the sliced cucumbers in the refrigerator
for up to 2 days. Cover with cling film or their flavour
will permeate other foods in the refrigerator.

# 炸洋葱餅

## Fried Onion Cakes

### INGREDIENTS (SERVES 4)

2 large onions
100 g/4 oz wheat flour
⅓ tspn salt
3 eggs
50 ml/2 fl oz water
9 tblspns corn oil

### SEASONING

1 tspn salt
¼ tblspn paprika

### METHOD

**1** Peel the onion, chop off end parts, then wash and slice finely.
**2** Mix together the wheat flour and salt, and then mix to a batter with the eggs, water and 1 tblspn oil.
**3** Heat 4 tblspns corn oil in a wok and stir-fry the sliced onions for 2 minutes. Remove with a slotted spoon, cool slightly, then mix with the batter.
**4** Heat the remaining oil in a frying pan and fry spoonfuls of the onion and batter, until golden brown on both sides.
**5** Mix the salt and paprika with 1 tblspn of the oil used for frying and serve with the hot onion cakes.

### NOTE

You could serve the onion cakes with tomato sauce instead of the paprika mix if you prefer.

# 炸紫菜素捲

## Crispy Laver Rolls

### INGREDIENTS (SERVES 4)

1 carrot
½ a cucumber
50 g/2 oz bamboo shoot
50 g/2 oz fungus
½ tspn salt
2 tblspns wheat flour
4½ tblspns water
3 pieces of laver
3 tblspns light soy sauce
2 tspns cornflour
½ tspn chilli powder
1½ tblspns corn oil

### METHOD

**1** Peel the carrot and shred finely. Wash the cucumber, peel and wash the bamboo shoot and wash the fungus. Shred all these vegetables finely. Put in a colander and sprinkle with the salt.
**2** Mix the wheat flour to a paste with 1½ tblspns water.
**3** Lay the pieces of laver out flat and arrange a third of the shredded vegetables on each piece as shown in the small picture 2. Roll up and seal the ends with the wheat flour paste.
**4** Put the soy sauce, cornflour, chilli powder and the remaining 3 tblspns water into a small saucepan. Bring to the boil, stirring, then remove from the heat.
**5** Heat the oil in a frying pan and fry the laver rolls over a medium heat for 5 minutes, turning them constantly. Remove, cut into diagonal pieces and serve with the soy sauce mixture.

干絲素麵

# Noodles of Dried Bean Curd Shreds

## INGREDIENTS (SERVES 2)

3 Chinese mushrooms
150 g/5 oz dried bean curd
    shreds
1.2 litres/2 pints boiling
    water
1 tspn bicarbonate soda
2 tblspns corn oil
1 tblspn shredded bamboo
    shoot
1 tblspn shredded carrot
1 tblspn shredded celery
1 tblspn straw mushrooms
450 ml/15 fl oz clear soup
    stock (see p. 116)

## SEASONING

⅔ tspn salt
2 tspns sesame oil

## METHOD

**1**   Soak the Chinese mushrooms for 20 minutes in boiling water. Drain. Cut off and discard the stalks and shred the caps.

**2**   Chop the dried bean curd shreds into sections and cook in the boiling water mixed with the bicarbonate of soda for 5 minutes. Drain and wash under cold running water.

**3**   Heat the oil in a wok and stir-fry the shredded Chinese mushrooms for 2 minutes. Add the bamboo shoot, carrot, celery and straw mushrooms and stir-fry for 3 minutes more. Add the seasoning and the soup. Bring to the boil, add the dried bean curd shreds, bring back to the boil and boil for 3 minutes. Serve at once.

## NOTE

Substitute 175 g/6 oz white vermicelli for the dried bean curd shreds.

# 凉拌海蜇

## Cold Blended Jellyfish

**INGREDIENTS** (SERVES 4)

450 g/1 lb jellyfish, shredded
½ tspn salt
2 tblspns light soy sauce
3 tblspns shredded carrot
3 tblspns shredded Chinese
  celery or spring onion
1 tspn sugar
1 tblspn sesame oil

**METHOD**

**1**  Cover the jellyfish with cold water and leave to soak for 20 minutes. Wash under cold running water, place in a colander and scald with boiling water. Immediately plunge into cold water and leave to soak for 4-5 hours (or until you want to serve it).
**2**  When ready to serve, drain the jellyfish and squeeze out the water. Mix the salt and half the soy sauce into the jelly fish and leave to stand for 10 minutes. Drain again very thoroughly.
**3**  Mix the jellyfish with the shredded carrot and Chinese celery or spring onion. Mix in the rest of the soy sauce with the sugar and sesame oil. Serve.

**NOTES**

**1**  You can use dried, fresh or frozen jellyfish for this recipe. Dried jellyfish must be soaked in cold water until it has softened. Frozen should be thoroughly defrosted before using.
**2**  When scalding the jellyfish, tip spoonfuls of boiling water over it rather than plunging it into a pan of boiling water. Stir the jellyfish as you pour on the water; the shreds should roll up.

# 黄瓜粉皮

## Cucumbers with Mung Bean Sheets

**INGREDIENTS** (SERVES 4)

3 cucumbers
2 tblspns crushed garlic
1 packet (about 8 slices)
  mung bean sheets

**SEASONING**
1 tblspn sesame oil
1½ tblspns white vinegar

**DRESSING**
2 tspns salt
2 tblspns sugar

**METHOD**

**1**  Wash the cucumbers; cut off the stalks and end pieces. Wipe them dry, then crush them slightly with the chopper. Chop into 2.5 cm/1-inch sections and mix with the garlic and dressing. Put into a bowl, cover with cling wrap and refrigerate for at least 4 hours.
**2**  Meanwhile, soak the mung bean sheets in cold water to soften them. Chop into 2.5 cm/1-inch sections.
**3**  Squeeze the juice from the cucumbers and mix with the strips of mung bean sheets. Stir in the seasoning and serve.

**NOTES**

**1**  If you like a hot taste, substitute chilli oil for the sesame oil and add 2 or 3 small chopped chillis.
**2**  Use mung bean sheets on the day that you buy them.

# 花生麵筋

## Peanut with Gluten Puff

### INGREDIENTS (SERVES 4)

150 g/5 oz raw peanuts
75 g/3 oz gluten puff
125 ml/4 fl oz water

### SEASONING
2 tblspns light soy sauce
½ tspn salt
½ tblspn rock sugar powder
1 tblspn brown sugar
2 star anises

### METHOD

**1** Wash the peanuts thoroughly and soak them in cold water for 4 hours.
**2** Put the gluten puff into a pan and cover with boiling water. Simmer until it is soft – about 5 minutes. Drain.
**3** Drain the peanuts and mix with the seasoning in a saucepan. Add the water and bring to the boil. Lower the heat and simmer for 10 minutes. Add the drained gluten puff and cook for 5 minutes more. Serve at once.

### NOTE
You can use cooked peanuts for this dish, in which case soak them first in boiling water containing 2-3 star anises for 1 hour (see small picture 3).

# 滷豆乾

## Spiced Bean Curds

### INGREDIENTS

1 pack of spices (see NOTES)
900 ml/1 pint water
275 g/10 oz spiced bean curds
2 tblspns light soy sauce
½ tblspn rock sugar

### METHOD

**1** Boil the pack of spices in the water for 30 minutes.
**2** Wash the spiced bean curds under cold running water. Add them to the pan with the soy sauce and the rock sugar. Bring to the boil, then lower the heat and simmer for 10 minutes. Remove from the heat, but leave the bean curds in the liquid until ready to serve.

### NOTES
**1** A pack of spices should contain star anise, fennel, dried orange peel, cinnamon and liquorice.
**2** If you do not cook the spiced bean curds on the day you have bought them, put them in a pan with some salt and cover with water. Bring to the boil and cook for 3 minutes. This will preserve them for up to 3 days. Keep in the refrigerator.

# 炒三色丁

## Stir-Fried Cubes in Three Colours

### INGREDIENTS (SERVES 4)

½ a salted cabbage, cubed
½ a preserved vegetable, cubed
4 tblspns corn oil
50 g/2 oz bamboo shoot, cubed

### SEASONING
1 tblspn sugar
½ tblspn light soy sauce
½ tspn white pepper
4 tblspns water

### METHOD

**1**  Soak the salted cabbage and preserved vegetable in cold water for 20 minutes. Drain well.
**2**  Heat the oil in a wok and stir-fry all the vegetables together for 1 minute. Add the seasoning, cover the pan and cook for 2 minutes. Serve.

### NOTES
**1**  This makes an ideal stuffing for steamed dumplings.
**2**  If you like, blend in 2 tspns sesame oil just before serving.

# 滷桶筍

## Marinated Bamboo Shoots

### INGREDIENTS (SERVES 6)

450 g/1 lb pickled bamboo shoots
2 star anises
2 red peppers, seeded
4 cloves garlic, finely chopped
4 tblspns corn oil
50-75 ml/2-3 fl oz water

### SEASONING
1 tspn salt
2 tblspns light soy sauce
1½ tblspns rock sugar powder

### METHOD

**1**  Tear the pickled bamboo shoots into long shreds. Wash them thoroughly, then squeeze out all the water.
**2**  Put the bamboo shreds into a saucepan and cover with water. Add the star anises, bring to the boil and boil for 5 minutes. Drain and rinse under running water. Squeeze out the water again.
**3**  Crush the peppers thoroughly with the back of the chopper then stir-fry with the garlic in the oil for 2 minutes. Add the bamboo shreds with the seasoning and the water. Stir for a few minutes, then simmer for about 20 minutes, stirring occasionally until the bamboo shoot is tender and most of the liquid has evaporated. Serve at once.

### NOTE
A large quantity of this dish can be prepared at one time as it will keep for up to 3 days in the refrigerator. Reheat as you want to serve it. This is why it is called *Marinated* Bamboo Shoots.

# 枸杞渾元

## Medlar with Egg

**INGREDIENTS** (SERVES 1)

4 tblspns fresh medlar leaves
300 ml/½ pint water or clear
    soup stock (see p. 116)
1 egg
⅓ tspn salt

**METHOD**

**1**  Pick the medlar leaves off the stems. Wash them and wipe dry on a clean cloth. Put into a soup bowl.
**2**  Put the water or soup into a small saucepan and bring it to the boil. Ladle out about 125 ml/4 fl oz and put this into a small bowl.
**3**  Break the egg into the small bowl and let it stand for about 30 seconds. Then stand the bowl in the saucepan of simmering liquid. Cook for 3-5 minutes until the white of the egg is setting. Pour the egg with the liquid over the medlar leaves. Add the salt and serve.

**NOTE**
Choose young tender medlar leaves for this dish; they will lose their bright green colour as soon as they come into contact with the boiling liquid.

# 奶蛋

## Steamed Milk Egg

**INGREDIENTS** (SERVES 1)

1 egg, beaten
150-175 ml/5-6 fl oz milk
1 tblspn castor sugar

**METHOD**

**1**  Strain the beaten egg, then stir in the milk and sugar. Pour into a small bowl.
**2**  Place the bowl in a steamer and steam, covered, over gently boiling water for 5 minutes. Remove the lid and steam for 5 minutes more. Serve.

**NOTE**
Use 1 tblspn honey instead of castor sugar.

# Spiced Sour Cabbage

**INGREDIENTS** (SERVES 4)

450 g/1 lb sour cabbage
4 tblspns corn oil
450 ml/¾ pint water or clear
    soup stock (see p. 116)

**SEASONING**
2 tblspns light soy sauce
1 tblspn rock sugar powder
1 tblspn brown sugar
½ tspn white pepper

**METHOD**

**1**   Wash the sour cabbage very thoroughly, discarding any old leaves. Squeeze out the liquid, then shred the cabbage and soak in cold water for 10 minutes. Drain.
**2**   Heat the oil in a wok. Mix the seasoning into the cabbage and stir-fry over a high heat for a few minutes. Add the water or soup stock, bring to the boil, then lower the heat, and simmer, covered, for 15 minutes, stirring occasionally. Drain off most of the liquid and serve at once.

**NOTES**
1   A large quantity of this dish can be prepared at one time as it will keep in the refrigerator for up to 5 days. Do not drain off the excess liquid until you heat it up to serve. The liquid helps to preserve the dish.
**2**   If you like a hot taste, add 2 finely chopped chillis to the seasoning ingredients.

# Marinated Chives

**INGREDIENTS** (SERVES 4)

275 g/10 oz chives
1½ tblspns salt

**SEASONING**
white wine vinegar
sesame oil

**METHOD**

**1**   Discard any old leaves from the chives. Wash the remainder and dry in a clean cloth.
**2**   Sprinkle the salt over the chives, then rub them with your hands until they have softened. Rinse the chives and squeeze out the liquid. Chop the chives finely and put into a dish.
**3**   Serve spoonfuls at a time, passing the white vinegar and sesame oil for each person to help themselves.

**NOTE**
This dish comes from northern China, where garlic is usually added to it.

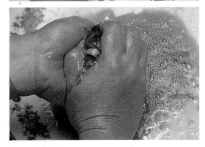

# Vegetarian Shark's Fins

## INGREDIENTS (SERVES 4)

25 g/1 oz fungus
1 bundle transparent
  vermicelli
4 Chinese mushrooms
2 green-stemmed flat
  cabbages
2 tblspns shredded bamboo
  shoot
2 tblspns shredded carrot
4 tblspns corn oil
2 tblspns water
900 ml/1½ pints clear soup
  stock (see p. 116)

### SEASONING A

1½ tspns salt
1 tblspn light soy sauce
½ tspn white pepper

### SEASONING B

1 tblspn cornflour mixed with
  2 tblspns water and 1 tspn
  sesame oil

## METHOD

**1**  Soak the fungus in cold water for 1 hour.
**2**  Soak the vermicelli in boiling water for 20 minutes. Drain and cut into even sections using scissors.
**3**  Soak the Chinese mushrooms in boiling water for 20 minutes. Drain, cut off and discard the stalks and shred the caps.
**4**  Cut away the root and withered outer leaves from the cabbages. Wash the leaves and chop into shreds.
**5**  Drain the fungus, then remove the stalk and chop the remainder into shreds.
**6**  Heat the oil in a wok and stir-fry all the prepared ingredients together with the 2 tblspns water. Add seasoning **A** and stir-fry for 2 minutes more.
**7**  Pour in the stock and bring to the boil. Stir in seasoning **B** and cook, stirring until the mixture thickens slightly. Serve at once.

## NOTE

**1**  The cooked transparent vermicelli resembles shark's fins, which is why the recipe has its name.
**2**  You can substitute 225 g/8 oz bean sprouts (see small picture 3, right) for the fungus.

# Long-Stem Mushrooms with Sesame Oil

## INGREDIENTS (SERVES 4)

450 g/1 lb long-stem
  mushrooms
salt
⅓ tblspn black sesame seeds
3 tblspns corn oil
1 tblspn ginger juice or 1½
  tblspns ginger wine

### SEASONING A

1 tspn salt
½ tblspn sesame oil

### SEASONING B

½ tblspn cornflour mixed
  with 3 tblspns water

## METHOD

**1**  Pick out any hard stems from the mushrooms (if using fresh ones), then chop off the root ends. Wash the mushrooms with water mixed with a little salt, then drain and wash again under cold running water. Drain well.
**2**  Pick out and discard any impurities in the black sesame seeds. Stir-fry the remainder with 1 tblspn oil over a gentle heat for 2 minutes. Tip onto a plate and rinse out the pan.
**3**  Put the oil and ginger juice or wine into the pan. Add the mushrooms and stir-fry for a minute or so. Add seasoning **A** and stir-fry for 2 minutes more.
**4**  Stir in seasoning **B**, and when the mixture has thickened, remove from the heat. Sprinkle with the black sesame seeds and serve.

# Soup of Five Blessings

**INGREDIENTS** (SERVES 4)

50 g/2 oz longan pulp
50 g/2 oz red dates
50 g/2 oz fresh lotus seeds
25-50 g/1-2 oz gingko fruits
25-50 g/1-2 oz fresh lily
1.2 litres/2 pints water
100 g/4 oz rock sugar,
    crushed

**METHOD**

**1**  Wash the longan pulp and the red dates. Soak the dates in cold water for 1-2 hours.
**2**  Wash the lotus seeds and the gingko fruits. Wash the lily and remove the outer membrane.
**3**  Put all the ingredients together with the water and crushed rock sugar into a saucepan. Bring to the boil, then lower the heat and simmer for 1 hour. Serve.

**NOTE**
If fresh lily and lotus seeds are not available, buy dried ones and soak them in cold water for 2-3 hours and overnight respectively.

# Lotus Root with Red Dates

**INGREDIENTS** (SERVES 4)

2 sections of lotus root
1 tspn salt
50 g/2 oz red dates, soaked
    overnight in cold water
25-50 g/1-2 oz rock sugar
900 ml/1½ pints water

**METHOD**

**1**  Peel the lotus root and chop it into bite-sized pieces. Wash thoroughly, adding the salt to the water. Drain.
**2**  Wash the red dates under running water after their soaking.
**3**  Put the lotus root pieces into a large saucepan with the dates, rock sugar and water. Bring to the boil, then lower the heat and simmer for 1-1½ hours until the mixture smells sweet. Keep an eye on the pan and add more water if it evaporates too much.

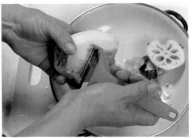

# 素酸辣湯
## Hot and Sour Soup

**INGREDIENTS** (SERVES 4)

4 Chinese mushrooms
1 tblspn dried black moss
3-4 red chillis
100 g/4 oz long-stem
   mushrooms
2 cakes of square bean curds
1 carrot
50 g/2 oz sour cabbage
6 tblspns corn oil
900 ml/1½ pints clear soup
   stock (see p. 116)
2 tblspns cornflour mixed
   with 4 tblspns water
1 egg, beaten

**SEASONING A**

2 tblspns dark soy sauce
1½ tspns salt
½ tspn white pepper

**SEASONING B**

4 tblspns brown vinegar
1 tblspn white vinegar
2 tspns sesame oil
1 tblspn chopped parsley

**METHOD**

**1**  Soak the Chinese mushrooms in boiling water for 20 minutes. Drain. Cut off and discard the stalks and shred the caps.
**2**  Soak the black moss for 20 minutes. Drain.
**3**  Wash the chillis and shred finely. Cut off and discard the roots from the long-stem mushrooms and wash.
**4**  Shred the bean curds. Peel the carrot and shred finely. Wash the sour cabbage and shred finely.
**5**  Heat the oil in a wok and stir-fry the Chinese mushrooms for 1 minute. Add all the other shredded ingredients and the long-stem mushrooms. Stir well, then add the soup stock and seasoning **A**. Bring to the boil and simmer for 2 minutes.
**6**  Stir in the cornflour mixture and bring to the boil, again, stirring until the soup thickens. Turn off the heat and leave for 1 minute, then stir in the beaten egg. Pour into a soup bowl and stir in seasoning **B**. Serve at once.

**NOTE**
If you cannot get long-stem mushrooms, use bean sprouts instead.

# 麻醬豆腐
## Bean Curds with Sesame Sauce

**INGREDIENTS** (SERVES 4)

4 cakes of square bean curds
900 ml/1½ pints water
1 tblspn finely chopped
   spring onion

**SEASONING**

1½ tblspns sesame sauce
1 tblspn sesame oil
1½ tblspns soy sauce
½ tspn salt
4 tblspns cold boiled water
1 tspn sugar

**METHOD**

**1**  Put the bean curds into a large saucepan with the water and bring to the boil for 1 minute. Drain and place in a deep plate.
**2**  Blend the seasoning together and pour it over the bean curds. Sprinkle with the spring onion and serve.

**NOTE**
For a different taste, add a small bunch of cedar shoots (see small picture 1 right) to the ingredients in this recipe. Rinse them in cold water, then drop into a pan of boiling water for 2 minutes and serve separately.

如意帶玉

# Stir-Fried Green Celery with Bean Sprouts

**INGREDIENTS** (SERVES 4)

450 g/1 lb bean sprouts
2 spiced bean curds
3 stalks Chinese celery
5 tblspns oil

**SEASONING**
1 tspn salt
1 tblspn light soy sauce
1 tblspn clear soup stock
   (see p. 116)
1 tspn sugar

**METHOD**

**1** Wash the bean sprouts and drain thoroughly. Chop the spiced bean curds into shreds.
**2** Cut off and discard the old stalks and leaves from the celery. Wash and cut into 2.5-cm/1-inch sections.
**3** Heat the oil in a wok and stir-fry the bean sprouts, bean curds and celery together with the seasoning for about 10 minutes. Cover and simmer for 2 minutes more, then serve.

堆金積玉

# Golden Glutens with Emerald Peppers

**INGREDIENTS** (SERVES 4)

225 g/8 oz gluten puff
2 tblspns dark soy sauce
6 green chillis
1 pan of corn oil for deep
   frying plus 4 tblspns extra
   oil

**SEASONING**
1 tspn salt
1 tblspn sugar
2 tblspns clear soup stock
   (see p. 116)

**METHOD**

**1** Chop the gluten puff into diagonal slices and marinate with the soy sauce for 20 minutes.
**2** Crush the green chillis gently with the chopper, then slice them into 2.5-cm/1-inch sections.
**3** Heat the pan of oil for deep frying and fry the gluten until browned. Remove with a slotted spoon and drain on absorbent paper.
**4** Heat the 4 tblspns oil in a wok and stir fry the chillis, fried glutens and seasoning over a high heat for 1 minute. Serve at once.

**NOTE**
If this dish is going to be too hot for you, substitute green peppers for the chillis.

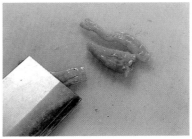

洋葱濃湯

# Onion Soup

## INGREDIENTS (SERVES 4)

2 small onions
1 slice bread
4 tblspns corn oil
600 ml/1 pint water

### SEASONING
1½ tspns salt
½ tblspn sugar
½ tspn black pepper

## METHOD

**1**  Peel the onions and cut off ends. Shred the remainder finely.
**2**  Toast the bread lightly and cut into cubes.
**3**  Heat the oil in a pan and stir-fry the onions until well browned. Add the water and bring to the boil. Lower the heat and simmer for 30 minutes. Add the seasoning and serve with the croûtons sprinkled on the surface.

## NOTE
If you want a creamy soup, use cream instead of oil to stir-fry the onions.

茄汁豆酥

# Beans with Tomato Sauce

## INGREDIENTS (SERVES 4)

275 g/10 oz peeled broad
    beans
100 g/4 oz wheat flour
⅓ tspn salt
⅓ tspn white pepper
1 egg white
4 tblspns corn oil
50 ml/2 fl oz water
1 pan of corn oil for deep
    frying
½ tblspn crushed garlic
3 tblspns tomato sauce or
    ketchup
4 tblspns water

### SEASONING
2 tblspns sugar
1 tblspn vinegar
1 tspn salt

## METHOD

**1**  Wash the beans and drain. Steam for 5 minutes.
**2**  Make a smooth batter with the wheat flour, salt, pepper, egg white, 1 tblspn oil and water. Add the beans to this and mix to coat them thoroughly.
**3**  Heat the oil for deep frying and drop in spoonfuls of the bean mixture, frying them until they are golden brown. Remove and drain on absorbent paper. Keep warm.
**4**  Heat the remaining 3 tblspns oil in a wok and stir-fry the garlic for 1 minute. Add the tomato sauce, water and seasoning and bring to the boil. Add the fried beans to this sauce, stirring to coat them evenly. Serve at once.

# Green-Stemmed Flat Cabbage with Chinese Mushrooms

### INGREDIENTS (SERVES 4)

8 large Chinese mushrooms
1 tsp salt
3 tblspns corn oil
450 g/1 lb green-stemmed
   flat cabbage
125 ml/4 fl oz clear soup
   stock (see p. 116)
1½ tblspns cornflour mixed
   with 1½ tblspns water

### SEASONING
1 tspn salt
1 tspn sugar

### METHOD

**1**   Soak the Chinese mushrooms in boiling water for 20 minutes. Drain. Cut off and discard the stalks and chop the caps in half.
**2**   Remove the outer withered leaves of the cabbage and wash the remainder. Chop into 6-cm/2½-inch pieces, then chop these in half lengthways. Blanch in boiling water mixed with the 1 tspn salt for 1-1½ minutes. Drain and soak in cold water until cold. Drain and squeeze out the water, then arrange the cabbage on a plate.
**3**   Heat the oil in a wok and stir-fry the mushrooms for 1-2 minutes. Add the stock and seasoning and cook for 5 minutes. Stir in the cornflour mixture and when the stock has thickened, spoon it and the mushrooms carefully over the cabbage. Serve at once.

# Shredded Water-Bamboo Shoots

### INGREDIENTS (SERVES 4)

275 g/10 oz water-bamboo
   shoots

### SEASONING
1 tspn salt
½ tblspn light soy sauce
½ tspn white pepper
3 tspns sesame oil
1 tspn sugar
1 tspn white vinegar

### METHOD

**1**   Cut away the outer skin of the water-bamboo shoots and chop off the end part. Slice each piece in half lengthways. Steam these pieces over boiling water for 12 minutes.
**2**   Remove from the steamer and shred the shoots finely. Mix with the seasoning and serve.

### NOTES
**1**   You can keep this in the refrigerator for up to 3 days. It makes a refreshing summer dish.
**2**   Substitute 275 g/10 oz shredded Chinese cabbage for the water-bamboo shoots.

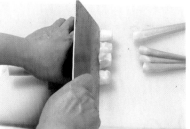

# 芝麻腐竹片
## Bean Curd Sheets with Black Sesame Seed

### INGREDIENTS

150 g/5 oz dried bean curd
   sheets
1 pan of corn oil for deep
   frying
1 tblspn black sesame seeds
1 tblspn corn oil
2 tblspns garlic soy sauce
   (see NOTES)

### METHOD

**1** Use scissors to cut the bean curd sheets into thin
strips and drop them, a few at a time, into the pan of
oil, heated until it is smoking. Fry until they turn
crispy. Remove and drain on absorbent paper while
you fry the remainder.
**2** Pick out and discard any impurities in the black
sesame seeds, then stir-fry them with the 1 tblspn oil
for 1-2 minutes over a gentle heat. Remove.
**3** Mix the garlic soy sauce with the fried bean curd
sheets and sprinkle the black sesame seeds over the
top.

### NOTE

To make garlic soy sauce, mix together 3 tblspns light
soy sauce, 1 tblspn crushed garlic and ½ tspn white
pepper. Keep in a screw-top jar.

# 蒜豉苦瓜
## Bitter Gourd with Fermented Beans

### INGREDIENTS (SERVES 4)

1 bitter gourd
½ tblspn salt
1 tblspn fermented black
   beans
6 tblspns corn oil
½ tblspn crushed garlic
½ tblspn finely chopped
   chillis
3 tblspns water

### SEASONING

1 tblspn soy sauce
½ tspn salt
1 tblspn sugar
½ tspn white pepper

### METHOD

**1** Chop the bitter gourd in half lengthways. Remove
the seeds and cut off the peel, the stalk and the end
part. Slice the flesh and sprinkle it with the salt. Leave
for 20 minutes, stirring the pieces with your hand
frequently, then squeeze out the juice. Blanch in
boiling water for 30 seconds and drain.
**2** Crush the fermented beans with the back of the
chopper.
**3** Heat the oil in a wok and stir-fry the beans, garlic
and chillis over a medium heat for 2-3 minutes. Add
the bitter gourd and stir everything together. Add the
seasoning and the water and simmer, covered, for 3-5
minutes. Serve.

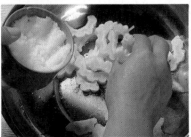

牡丹富貴

# Stewed Cabbage with Mixed Vegetables

## INGREDIENTS (SERVES 4)

2-3 Chinese mushrooms
50 g/2 oz bamboo·shoot
1 medium Chinese cabbage
900 ml/1½ pints clear
    soup stock (see p. 116)
1½ tblspns carrot (diced)
1½ tblspns corn kernels
1½ tblspns green beans
1½ tblspns preserved
    vegetable

## SEASONING
1½ tspns salt
½ tspn white pepper

## METHOD

**1**  Soak the Chinese mushrooms in boiling water for 20 minutes. Drain. Cut off and discard the stalks. Shred the bamboo shoot and soak in cold water.
**2**  Cut off and discard any old or withered leaves and the root part from the cabbage. Wash the leaves and shred them.
**3**  Put the soup stock into a large saucepan with the cabbage. Sprinkle all the other vegetables on top. Add the seasoning, bring to boiling point over a medium heat, then lower the heat and simmer very gently for 30 minutes. Serve at once.

## NOTE
If you like you could sprinkle 2 finely chopped spring onions over the soup just before serving.

鉄板豆腐

# Fried Bean Curds with Onions

### INGREDIENTS (SERVES 4)

3 cakes bean curds
1 onion
3 red chillis
4 garlic cloves, crushed
2 tblspns Hoisin sauce
4 tblspns corn oil
1 tblspn cornflour mixed with
    2 tblspns water
3 spring onions

### SEASONING A

1½ tspns salt
1 tblspn soy sauce
½ tblspn sugar
3 tblspns clear soup stock
    (see p. 116)

### SEASONING B

½ tblspn dry sherry
½ tblspn brown vinegar
1 tspn black pepper

### METHOD

**1**   Put the bean curds into a saucepan and cover
with water. Bring to the boil over a medium heat for
3-5 minutes. Then drain and cut into 2.5-cm/1-inch
cubes.
**2**   Peel the onion and cut off the ends. Slice thinly.
Wash the chillis and chop finely.
**3**   Blend seasoning **A** with the chopped chillis,
crushed garlic and Hoisin sauce. Heat the oil in a wok
and stir-fry this mixture for a few seconds, then add
the bean curd cubes. Stir over a medium heat until
they are well coated with the sauce, then lower the
heat and simmer, covered for 5-10 minutes.
**4**   Remove the lid and add the sliced onion and
seasoning **B**. Turn up the heat and cook, stirring, for
1½ minutes.
**5**   Stir in the cornflour mixture to thicken and serve
sprinkled with the spring onion cut in diagonal slices.

### NOTE

If you have an iron plate, heat it until it is very hot and
serve this dish on it. The ingredients should 'hiss' as
you spoon them onto the iron plate.

# Clear Soup Stock

## INGREDIENTS

175 g/6 oz parsnips
175 g/6 oz turnips
2 onions
4 celery stalks
2 tblspns corn oil
4 tblspns chopped button
    mushroom stalks
1.5 litres/2½ pints water
2 tspns salt
bouquet garni (see NOTES)
3 black peppercorns

## METHOD

**1**  Wash the parsnips and turnips but do not peel.
Chop them into chunks. Peel the onions, wash the
celery and chop these into chunks, too.
**2**  Heat the oil in a large saucepan and add all the
chopped vegetables and the mushroom stalks. Cook,
stirring occasionally, for 5-7 minutes over a medium
heat.
**3**  Add the water, salt, bouquet garni and
peppercorns to the pan. Bring to the boil, then lower
the heat and simmer for 30 minutes.
**4**  Strain the liquid into a bowl, pressing the
vegetables with the back of a wooden spoon to
extract as much liquid as possible. Discard the
vegetables left in the strainer.
**5**  Let the stock cool completely, then cover with
cling wrap and put in the refrigerator.

## NOTES

**1**  Make a bouquet garni by tying together 2 sprigs of
parsley, 1 sprig of thyme and 1 bay leaf.
**2**  Keep the stock for 2-3 days in the refrigerator, or
freeze it in small quantities (ice-cube trays or small
yoghurt cartons make ideal containers) and use as
required.

# Rich Soup Stock

## INGREDIENTS

100 g/4 oz carrots
100 g/4 oz turnips
100 g/4 oz button mushrooms
2 onions
4 celery stalks
100 g/4 oz tomatoes
2 tblspns corn oil
1.5 litres/2½ pints water
2 tspns salt
bouquet garni (see NOTES
    above)
3 black peppercorns

## METHOD

**1**  Wash the carrots and turnips but do not peel.
Wipe the mushrooms with damp absorbent paper.
Peel the onions and wash the celery and the
tomatoes. Chop all these vegetables into chunks.
**2**  Heat the oil in a large saucepan and add all the
chopped vegetables. Cook, stirring occasionally, for
8-10 minutes, over a medium heat.
**3**  Add the water, salt, bouquet garni and
peppercorns to the pan. Bring to the boil, then lower
the heat and simmer for 30 minutes.
**4**  Finish off as outlined above in Clear Soup Stock.

# Glossary

**Angled Luffa**
This is a summer vegetable gourd and will only be found in Chinese supermarkets during the summer months. It has a sweet flavour and can be used to make soup or a kind of cake, as well as being used in stir-fried dishes. It may also be known as Chinese okra or silk squash.

**Bean Curd Sheets**
Bean Curd Sheets are available at all Chinese supermarkets; they need to be soaked for 20-30 minutes before using to soften them. Some stores also stock fresh bean curd skins, which can generally be used in place of the sheets. They do not need soaking before use.

**Bitter Gourd**
Bitter gourd, also known as bitter melon, is generally available from Chinese supermarkets throughout the summer months. Look for those that are a good round shape with a rough skin and a clear white colour. Rubbing salt into the cut flesh helps to lessen the bitter taste.

**Black Moss**
Black Moss is a kind of seaweed, and like all seaweeds, it is highly nutritious.

**Chayoto**
Chayoto is a vegetable only available in Chinese supermarkets in the spring. Look for those that are smooth and young – they are tastier and more tender than the older, rougher-skinned ones.

**Chinese Mushrooms**
Chinese Mushrooms are dried and will either be black in colour, or a very dark brown with white markings. The best quality ones will be even-sized with thick caps, and their flavour is quite distinct from all other mushrooms. They must be soaked in boiling water for 20 minutes or cold water for 1 hour before using in a recipe.

**Five-Spice Powder**
This is a popular flavouring in Chinese dishes. It has a strong flavour and consists of ground star anise, cloves, fennel, peppercorns and cinnamon.

**Fresh Lily**
These are the gold-coloured buds of the tiger-lily and will sometimes be available fresh. They are also known as day lily. When not available, use the dried ones and soak them overnight in cold water. They are a perfectly acceptable substitute, but they do have a slightly sourer taste.

**Fungus**
Fungus is available at Chinese supermarkets. Known also as wood, it may be black, white or brown in colour and is quite expensive.

**Fuzzy Melons**
Fuzzy melons are only available in Chinese supermarkets during the summer months. You can generally substitute cucumbers for fuzzy melons in most recipes, but of course, the flavour will be different.

**Gluten Puff**
This can be bought frozen from most Chinese supermarkets. It should be thawed completely before using. If frozen is not available, canned glutens could be used, but they are usually marinated in a sauce which may not complement the recipe.

**Hoisin Sauce**
Available at Chinese supermarkets, this sweet-tasting sauce is also known as Barbecue sauce.

**Lotus Root**
Fresh lotus root is available during the summer months at Chinese supermarkets. Canned lotus root can usually be used when the fresh is not available.

**Medlar Leaves**
Medlar leaves will only be available at Chinese supermarkets. If they are not available, there is really no satisfactory substitute. They are said to be a good tonic for the liver and kidneys.

**Preserved Vegetables**
Preserved vegetables are available in 175 g/6 oz and 350 g/12 oz cans. The ingredients are Chinese radish, spices, salt and chilli. Once opened, the vegetables can be kept for up to 3 months in a dry container. Rinse under cold running water before using.

**Red Dates**
Red dates are also known as red jujubes. They are fragrant and sweet, and attributed with nourishing the blood and beautifying the skin.

**Straw Mushrooms**
These may be sold fresh or canned. Fresh ones last only a few days; canned ones can be kept for up to one week in the refrigerator after opening, if covered with cold water, which must be changed daily.

**Water Chestnuts**
Fresh water chestnuts are sometimes available at Chinese supermarkets. In all the recipes in this book where water chestnuts are used, canned ones would be perfectly suitable.

**Wonton Skins**
These pliable skins are made from a dough of a special high-gluten flour and eggs. They may be sold fresh or frozen. Fresh ones will keep for up to a week in the refrigerator. Keep in a plastic container.

**White Fungus**
Two kinds of white fungus are available; one is pure white and the other slightly yellow in colour. The former looks more attractive, but the latter is superior in nutritive value. Both are said to strengthen the lungs, beautify the complexion and improve masculine virility.

**White Wormwood**
White wormwood is available at Chinese supermarkets. Besides being used in stir-fried dishes, it can be used to make soup or stuffing.

Unless otherwise stated, the sugar used in the recipes in this book is granulated sugar.

## KEY TO VEGETABLES AND INGREDIENTS

Many of the vegetables illustrated here will be known to you; others are perhaps currently less identifiable. Not all of them appear in the recipes in this book, but you can use this guide to help you to identify the unknown vegetables you encounter during your forays into Chinese supermarkets.

1. Cabbage
2. Mustard Greens
3. White Chinese Cabbage
4. Fennel
5. Watercress
6. Chinese Spinach
7. Chives
8. Chinese Chives

9. Lettuce
10. Brussels Sprouts
11. White Wormwood
12. Chinese Flat Cabbage
13. Pea Shoots
14. Chinese Cress
15. Stem Lettuce
16. Red Leaves
17. Sweet Potato Leaves

18. Asparagus
19. Chou-Tu-Fu (Bean Curd)
20. Lotus Leaf
21. Chinese Cabbage
22. Fuzzy Melon
23. Pickled Bamboo Shoots
24. Angled Luffa

25. Pickled Melon
26. Pickled Cowpea
27. Cedar Shoots
28. Sour Cabbage
29. Salted Vegetable
30. Taro Stalk

31. Mustard Flower
32. Kale
33. Celery
34. Rape Flower
35. Bitter Gourd
36. Green-stemmed Flat Cabbage
37. Spinach
38. Aubergines

39. Bottle Gourd
40. Large Cucumber
41. Turnip
42. Green Oriental Radish
43. Kale Flower
44. Red Radish
45. Red Peppers (Bell Peppers)
46. Cucumber

47. White Chinese Cabbage
48. Leek
49. Green Peppers
50. Carrot
51. Garlic Stem
52. Medlar
53. Corns
54. Winter Melon

55. Water Spinach
56. Mustard Stem
57. Chinese Greens
58. *Ma* Bamboo Shoots
59. Garlic Flower
60. Lotus Root
61. Uzura Beans
62. Sponge Gourd
63. Taro

64. Chinese Mallow
65. Water-Bamboo
66. Basil
67. *Kuei* Bamboo Shoots
68. Green Bamboo
    Shoots
69. Taro
70. Chinese Yam
71. Burdock
72. Tomato
73. Chinese Mushrooms

74. Pumpkin
75. White Yam
76. Bean Sprouts
77. Sweet Potatoes
78. Potatoes
79. Bur Clover
80. Rape (Field Mustard)
81. Broccoli
82. Cauliflower
83. Yam Bean
84. Mange Touts

85. Green Peas
86. Lima Beans
87. Green Beans
88. Baby Corn Shoots
89. Straw Mushrooms
90. Button Mushrooms
91. Jack Beans
92. Water Chestnuts
93. Kohlrabi
94. Bamboo Shoots
95. Abalone Mushrooms

96. Arrow Head
97. Long-stem
    Mushrooms
98. Fungus
99. Chayotoes
100. Leaf Beet
101. Broad Beans
102. String Beans

# Index

# Stockists

Cheong Leen
4-10 Tower Street
London WC2H 9NR
Tel: (01) 836 5378

Osaka Limited
17-17a Goldhurst Terrace
Finchley Road
London NW6 3HX
Tel: (01) 624 4983

Loon Fung Supermarket
41-42 Gerrard Street
London W1V 7LP
Tel: (01) 437 1922

Hong Kong Supermarket
93 Shaftsbury Avenue
London W1V 7AE
Tel: (01) 734 2857

Chinese Food Centre Ltd
156 Balham High Road
London SW12 8BN
Tel: (01) 675 3120

Sheen Road Food Stores
116 Sheen Road
Richmond
Surrey
Tel: (01) 948 6805

S.W. Trading
283 Water Road
Alperton
Middlesex HA0 1HX
Tel: (01) 998 2248

Eastern Stores
214-216 Kingston Road
Portsmouth PO2 7LR
Tel: (0705) 662816

Continental Food Centre
148 Cornwall Street
Plymouth PL1 1NJ
Tel: (0752) 669073

Kam Cheun
Chinese Supermarket
28-30 Burleigh Street
Cambridge CB1 1DG
Tel: (0223) 316429

Janson Hong Kong
Chinese Supermarket
17-18 St Martin's House
Bull Ring
Birmingham B5 5DD
Tel: (021) 643 4681

PKM Chinese Co Ltd
5 Melton Street
Leicester LE1 3NA
Tel: (0533) 29656

Chung Wai Trading Co.
31-32 Great George Square
Liverpool L1 5DZ
Tel: (051) 709 2637

Man Cheong Hong
99 Fishergate Hill
Preston
Lancashire
Tel: (0772) 22509

Tai Sun Chinese Supermarket
49 College Road
Balby
Doncaster
South Yorkshire
Tel: (1302) 4360

Jim's Chinese Supermarket
7a Bath Street
Glasgow G2
Tel: (041) 342 4492